Cram101 Textbook Outlines to accompany:

Psychological Testing

Anastasi and Urbina, 7th Edition

An Academic Internet Publishers (AIPI) publication (c) 2007.

You have a discounted membership at www.Cram101.com with this book.

Get all of the practice tests for the chapters of this textbook, and access in-depth reference material for writing essays and papers. Here is an example from a Cram101 Biology text:

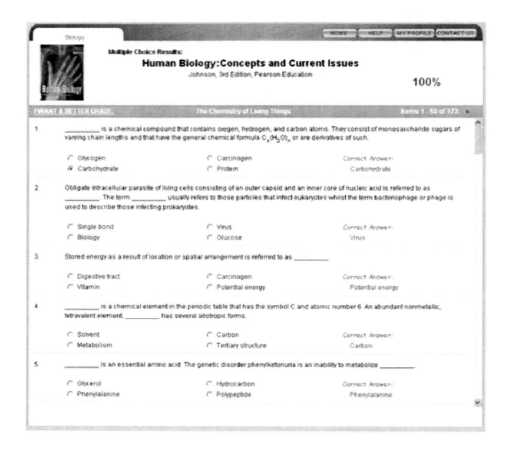

When you need problem solving help with math, stats, and other disciplines, www.Cram101.com will walk through the formulas and solutions step by step.

With Cram101.com online, you also have access to extensive reference material.

You will nail those essays and papers. Here is an example from a Cram101 Biology text:

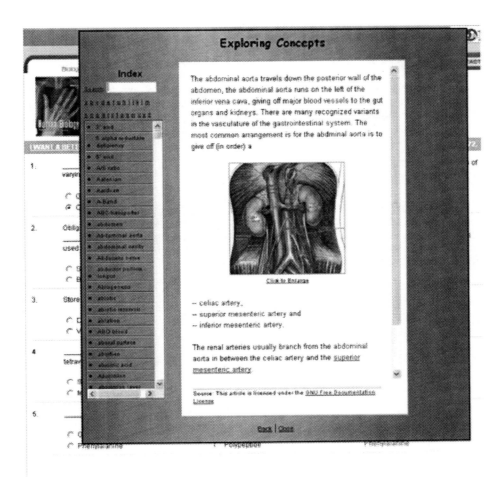

Learning System

Cram101 Textbook Outlines is a learning system. The notes in this book are the highlights of your textbook, you will never have to highlight a book again.

How to use this book. Take this book to class, it is your notebook for the lecture. The notes and highlights on the left hand side of the pages follow the outline and order of the textbook. All you have to do is follow along while your intructor presents the lecture. Circle the items emphasized in class and add other important information on the right side. With Cram101 Textbook Outlines you'll spend less time writing and more time listening. Learning becomes more efficient.

Cram101.com Online

Increase your studying efficiency by using Cram101.com's practice tests and online reference material. It is the perfect complement to Cram101 Textbook Outlines. Use self-teaching matching tests or simulate in-class testing with comprehensive multiple choice tests, or simply use Cram's true and false tests for quick review. Cram101.com even allows you to enter your in-class notes for an integrated studying format combining the textbook notes with your class notes.

Psychological Testing
Anastasi and Urbina, 7th

CONTENTS

Psychological test	Psychological test refers to a standardized measure of a sample of a person's behavior.
Construct	A generalized concept, such as anxiety or gravity, is a construct.
Psychological testing	Psychological testing is a field characterized by the use of small samples of behavior in order to infer larger generalizations about a given individual. The technical term for psychological testing is psychometrics.
Basic research	Basic research has as its primary objective the advancement of knowledge and the theoretical understanding of the relations among variables . It is exploratory and often driven by the researcher's curiosity, interest or hunch.
Psychotherapy	Psychotherapy is a set of techniques based on psychological principles intended to improve mental health, emotional or behavioral issues.
Variable	A variable refers to a measurable factor, characteristic, or attribute of an individual or a system.
Trait	An enduring personality characteristic that tends to lead to certain behaviors is called a trait. The term trait also means a genetically inherited feature of an organism.
Empirical	Empirical means the use of working hypotheses which are capable of being disproved using observation or experiment.
Aptitude test	A test designed to predict a person's ability in a particular area or line of work is called an aptitude test.
Projective personality test	A method in which a person is shown an ambiguous stimulus and asked to describe it or tell a story about it is called a projective personality test.
Personality test	A personality test aims to describe aspects of a person's character that remain stable across situations.
Personality	Personality refers to the pattern of enduring characteristics that differentiates a person, the patterns of behaviors that make each individual unique.
Rorschach	The Rorschach inkblot test is a method of psychological evaluation. It is a projective test associated with the Freudian school of thought. Psychologists use this test to try to probe the unconscious minds of their patients.
Mental retardation	Mental retardation refers to having significantly below-average intellectual functioning and limitations in at least two areas of adaptive functioning. Many categorize retardation as mild, moderate, severe, or profound.
Learning	Learning is a relatively permanent change in behavior that results from experience. Thus, to attribute a behavioral change to learning, the change must be relatively permanent and must result from experience.
Independent variable	A condition in a scientific study that is manipulated (assigned different values by a researcher) so that the effects of the manipulation may be observed is called an independent variable.
Norms	In testing, standards of test performance that permit the comparison of one person's score on the test to the scores of others who have taken the same test are referred to as norms.
Representative sample	Representative sample refers to a sample of participants selected from the larger population in such a way that important subgroups within the population are included in the sample in the same proportions as they are found in the larger population.
Normative	The term normative is used to describe the effects of those structures of culture which regulate the function of social activity.

Reliability	Reliability means the extent to which a test produces a consistent , reproducible score .
Validity	The extent to which a test measures what it is intended to measure is called validity.
Psychometric	Psychometric study is concerned with the theory and technique of psychological measurement, which includes the measurement of knowledge, abilities, attitudes, and personality traits. The field is primarily concerned with the study of differences between individuals
Test reliability	Test Reliability is the extent to which a test is repeatable and yields consistent scores.
Correlation	A statistical technique for determining the degree of association between two or more variables is referred to as correlation.
Scholastic Assessment Test	The Scholastic Assessment Test is a standardized test frequently used by colleges and universities to aid in the selection of incoming students.
Intelligence test	An intelligence test is a standardized means of assessing a person's current mental ability, for example, the Stanford-Binet test and the Wechsler Adult Intelligence Scale.
IQ test	An IQ test is a standardized test developed to measure a person's cognitive abilities ("intelligence") in relation to their age group.
Innate	Innate behavior is not learned or influenced by the environment, rather, it is present or predisposed at birth.
Attention	Attention is the cognitive process of selectively concentrating on one thing while ignoring other things. Psychologists have labeled three types of attention: sustained attention, selective attention, and divided attention.
Survey	A method of scientific investigation in which a large sample of people answer questions about their attitudes or behavior is referred to as a survey.
Color blindness	Color blindness in humans is the inability to perceive differences between some or all colors that other people can distinguish. It is most often of genetic nature, but may also occur because of eye, nerve, or brain damage, or due to exposure to certain chemicals.
Anxiety	Anxiety is a complex combination of the feeling of fear, apprehension and worry often accompanied by physical sensations such as palpitations, chest pain and/or shortness of breath.
Generalization	In conditioning, the tendency for a conditioned response to be evoked by stimuli that are similar to the stimulus to which the response was conditioned is a generalization. The greater the similarity among the stimuli, the greater the probability of generalization.
Variance	The degree to which scores differ among individuals in a distribution of scores is the variance.
Generalizability	The ability to extend a set of findings observed in one piece of research to other situations and groups is called generalizability.
Population	Population refers to all members of a well-defined group of organisms, events, or things.
Affect	A subjective feeling or emotional tone often accompanied by bodily expressions noticeable to others is called affect.
Standardized test	An oral or written assessment for which an individual receives a score indicating how the individual reponded relative to a previously tested large sample of others is referred to as a standardized test.
Test norms	Test norms are standards that provide information about where a score on a psychological test ranks in relation to other scores on that test .
Behavioral observation	A form of behavioral assessment that entails careful observation of a person's overt behavior in a particular situation is behavioral observation.
Projective test	A projective test is a personality test designed to let a person respond to ambiguous stimuli,

Go to **Cram101.com** for the Practice Tests for this Chapter.

presumably revealing hidden emotions and internal conflicts. This is different from an "objective test" in which responses are analyzed according to a universal standard rather than an individual psychiatrist's judgement.

Shyness	A tendency to avoid others plus uneasiness and strain when socializing is called shyness.
Individual intelligence test	A test of intelligence designed to be given to a single individual by a trained specialist is an individual intelligence test. Background information supplements the test.
Socioeconomic Status	A family's socioeconomic status is based on family income, parental education level, parental occupation, and social status in the community. Those with high status often have more success in preparing their children for school because they have access to a wide range of resources.
Socioeconomic	Socioeconomic pertains to the study of the social and economic impacts of any product or service offering, market intervention or other activity on an economy as a whole and on the companies, organization and individuals who are its main economic actors.
Ethnicity	Ethnicity refers to a characteristic based on cultural heritage, nationality characteristics, race, religion, and language.
Perception	Perception is the process of acquiring, interpreting, selecting, and organizing sensory information.
Control group	A group that does not receive the treatment effect in an experiment is referred to as the control group or sometimes as the comparison group.
Reasoning	Reasoning is the act of using reason to derive a conclusion from certain premises. There are two main methods to reach a conclusion,deductive reasoning and inductive reasoning.
Feedback	Feedback refers to information returned to a person about the effects a response has had.
Test anxiety	High levels of arousal and worry that seriously impair test performance is referred to as test anxiety.
Individual differences	Individual differences psychology studies the ways in which individual people differ in their behavior. This is distinguished from other aspects of psychology in that although psychology is ostensibly a study of individuals, modern psychologists invariably study groups.
Questionnaire	A self-report method of data collection or clinical assessment method in which the individual being studied checks off items on a printed list, answers multiple-choice questions, or writes out answers to essay questions aimed at producing a selfdescription is called questionnaire.
Attitude	An enduring mental representation of a person, place, or thing that evokes an emotional response and related behavior is called attitude.
Negative correlation	A negative correlation refers to a relationship between two variables in which one variable increases as the other decreases.
Achievement test	A test designed to determine a person's level of knowledge in a given subject area is referred to as an achievement test.
Zimbardo	Zimbardo is best-known for his Stanford prison experiment. The experiment led to theories about the importance of the social situation in individual psychology that are still controversial today.
Ego	In Freud's view the Ego serves to balance our primitive needs and our moral beliefs and taboos. Relying on experience, a healthy Ego provides the ability to adapt to reality and interact with the outside world.
Acquisition	Acquisition is the process of adapting to the environment, learning or becoming conditioned. In classical conditoning terms, it is the initial learning of the stimulus response link, which involves a neutral stimulus being associated with a unconditioned stimulus and becoming a conditioned stimulus.
Retrieval	Retrieval is the location of stored information and its subsequent return to consciousness. It is the

third stage of information processing.

Stereotype	A stereotype is considered to be a group concept, held by one social group about another. They are often used in a negative or prejudicial sense and are frequently used to justify certain discriminatory behaviors. This allows powerful social groups to legitimize and protect their dominant position
Habit	A habit is a response that has become completely separated from its eliciting stimulus. Early learning theorists used the term to describe S-R associations, however not all S-R associations become a habit, rather many are extinguished after reinforcement is withdrawn.
Motivation	In psychology, motivation is the driving force (desire) behind all actions of an organism.
Intellectually gifted	Intellectually gifted refers to having an IQ score above 130; about 2 to 4 percent of the population.
Test battery	A group of tests and interviews given to the same individual is a test battery.
American Psychological Association	The American Psychological Association is a professional organization representing psychology in the US. The mission statement is to "advance psychology as a science and profession and as a means of promoting health, education , and human welfare".
Society	The social sciences use the term society to mean a group of people that form a semi-closed (or semi-open) social system, in which most interactions are with other individuals belonging to the group.

Psychological testing	Psychological testing is a field characterized by the use of small samples of behavior in order to infer larger generalizations about a given individual. The technical term for psychological testing is psychometrics.
Antecedents	In behavior modification, events that typically precede the target response are called antecedents.
Infancy	The developmental period that extends from birth to 18 or 24 months is called infancy.
Mental retardation	Mental retardation refers to having significantly below-average intellectual functioning and limitations in at least two areas of adaptive functioning. Many categorize retardation as mild, moderate, severe, or profound.
Intelligence test	An intelligence test is a standardized means of assessing a person's current mental ability, for example, the Stanford-Binet test and the Wechsler Adult Intelligence Scale.
Discrimination	In Learning theory, discrimination refers the ability to distinguish between a conditioned stimulus and other stimuli. It can be brought about by extensive training or differential reinforcement. In social terms, it is the denial of privileges to a person or a group on the basis of prejudice.
Attention	Attention is the cognitive process of selectively concentrating on one thing while ignoring other things. Psychologists have labeled three types of attention: sustained attention, selective attention, and divided attention.
Individual differences	Individual differences psychology studies the ways in which individual people differ in their behavior. This is distinguished from other aspects of psychology in that although psychology is ostensibly a study of individuals, modern psychologists invariably study groups.
Generalization	In conditioning, the tendency for a conditioned response to be evoked by stimuli that are similar to the stimulus to which the response was conditioned is a generalization. The greater the similarity among the stimuli, the greater the probability of generalization.
Variability	Statistically, variability refers to how much the scores in a distribution spread out, away from the mean.
Experimental psychology	Experimental psychology is an approach to psychology that treats it as one of the natural sciences, and therefore assumes that it is susceptible to the experimental method.
Physiology	The study of the functions and activities of living cells, tissues, and organs and of the physical and chemical phenomena involved is referred to as physiology.
Reaction time	The amount of time required to respond to a stimulus is referred to as reaction time.
Brightness	The dimension of visual sensation that is dependent on the intensity of light reflected from a surface and that corresponds to the amplitude of the light wave is called brightness.
Stimulus	A change in an environmental condition that elicits a response is a stimulus.
Launching	The process in which youths move into adulthood and exit their family of origin is called launching. It can be a time to formulate life goals, to develop an identity, and to become more independent before joining with another person to form a new family.
Galton	Galton was one of the first experimental psychologists, and the founder of the field of Differential Psychology, which concerns itself with individual differences rather than on common trends. He created the statistical methods correlation and regression.
Heredity	Heredity is the transfer of characteristics from parent to offspring through their genes.
Kraepelin	Kraepelin postulated that there is a specific brain or other biological pathology underlying each of the major psychiatric disorders. Just as his laboratory discovered the pathologic basis of what is now known as Alzheimers disease, Kraepelin was confident that it would

	someday be possible to identify the pathologic basis of each of the major psychiatric disorders.
Practice effects	Practice effects are the effects brought about by the continued repetition of a task.
Memory span	The second key concept associated with a short-term memory is that it has a finite capacity. Prior to the creation of current memory models, George Miller argued that human short-term memory has a forward memory span of approximately seven items plus or minus two.
Ebbinghaus	Ebbinghaus pioneered the development of experimental methods for the measurement of rote learning and memory.
Reasoning	Reasoning is the act of using reason to derive a conclusion from certain premises. There are two main methods to reach a conclusion, deductive reasoning and inductive reasoning.
Mental age	The mental age refers to the accumulated months of credit that a person earns on the Stanford-Binet Intelligence Scale.
Adaptation	Adaptation is a lowering of sensitivity to a stimulus following prolonged exposure to that stimulus. Behavioral adaptations are special ways a particular organism behaves to survive in its natural habitat.
Intelligence quotient	An intelligence quotient is a score derived from a set of standardized tests that were developed with the purpose of measuring a person's cognitive abilities ("intelligence") in relation to their age group.
Chronological age	Chronological age refers to the number of years that have elapsed since a person's birth.
Stanford-Binet	Terman released the "Stanford Revision of the Binet-Simon Scale" or the Stanford-Binet for short. Using validation experiments, he removed several of the Binet-Simon test items and added new ones. In 1985 it was revised to analyze an individual's responses in four content areas: verbal reasoning, quantitative reasoning, abstract reasoning, and short-term memory.
Terman	Terman revised the Stanford-Binet Intelligence Scale in 1916, commonly used to measure intelligence (or I.Q.) in the United States. William Stern's suggestion that mental age/chronological age times 100 (to get rid of the decimal) be made the "intelligence quotient" or I.Q. This apparent mathematization of the measurement gave it an air of scientific accuracy and detachment which contributed greatly to its acceptance among educators and the broad public.
Clinician	A health professional authorized to provide services to people suffering from one or more pathologies is a clinician.
Insight	Insight refers to a sudden awareness of the relationships among various elements that had previously appeared to be independent of one another.
Aptitude test	A test designed to predict a person's ability in a particular area or line of work is called an aptitude test.
Trait	An enduring personality characteristic that tends to lead to certain behaviors is called a trait. The term trait also means a genetically inherited feature of an organism.
Factor analysis	Factor analysis is a statistical technique that originated in psychometrics. The objective is to explain the most of the variability among a number of observable random variables in terms of a smaller number of unobservable random variables called factors.
Thurstone	Thurstone was a pioneer in the field of psychometrics. His work in factor analysis led him to formulate a model of intelligence center around "Primary Mental Abilities", which were independent group factors of intelligence that different individuals possessed in varying degrees.

Spatial visualization	An aspect of spatial cognition that involves the mental manipulations of visual stimuli, such as performing mental rotation or solving embedded-figures problems is referred to as spatial visualization.
Achievement test	A test designed to determine a person's level of knowledge in a given subject area is referred to as an achievement test.
Standardized test	An oral or written assessment for which an individual receives a score indicating how the individual reponded relative to a previously tested large sample of others is referred to as a standardized test.
Thorndike	Thorndike worked in animal behavior and the learning process leading to the theory of connectionism. Among his most famous contributions were his research on cats escaping from puzzle boxes, and his formulation of the Law of Effect.
Normative	The term normative is used to describe the effects of those structures of culture which regulate the function of social activity.
Psychometric	Psychometric study is concerned with the theory and technique of psychological measurement, which includes the measurement of knowledge, abilities, attitudes, and personality traits. The field is primarily concerned with the study of differences between individuals
Personality test	A personality test aims to describe aspects of a person's character that remain stable across situations.
Personality	Personality refers to the pattern of enduring characteristics that differentiates a person, the patterns of behaviors that make each individual unique.
Motivation	In psychology, motivation is the driving force (desire) behind all actions of an organism.
Attitude	An enduring mental representation of a person, place, or thing that evokes an emotional response and related behavior is called attitude.
Free association	In psychoanalysis, the uncensored uttering of all thoughts that come to mind is called free association.
Mental disorder	Mental disorder refers to a disturbance in a person's emotions, drives, thought processes, or behavior that involves serious and relatively prolonged distress and/or impairment in ability to function, is not simply a normal response to some event or set of events in the person's environment.
Questionnaire	A self-report method of data collection or clinical assessment method in which the individual being studied checks off items on a printed list, answers multiple-choice questions, or writes out answers to essay questions aimed at producing a selfdescription is called questionnaire.
Prototype	A concept of a category of objects or events that serves as a good example of the category is called a prototype.
Psychopathology	Psychopathology refers to the field concerned with the nature and development of mental disorders.
Woodworth Personal Data Sheet	The first modern personality test was the Woodworth Personal Data Sheet first used in 1919. It was designed to help the United States Army screen out recruits who might be susceptible to shell shock.
Affective	Affective is the way people react emotionally, their ability to feel another living thing's pain or joy.

Go to **Cram101.com** for the Practice Tests for this Chapter.

Reliability	Reliability means the extent to which a test produces a consistent, reproducible score.
Validity	The extent to which a test measures what it is intended to measure is called validity.
Norms	In testing, standards of test performance that permit the comparison of one person's score on the test to the scores of others who have taken the same test are referred to as norms.
Psychological test	Psychological test refers to a standardized measure of a sample of a person's behavior.
Raw score	A raw score is an original datum that has not been transformed – for example, the original result obtained by a student on a test (i.e., the number of correctly answered items) as opposed to that score after transformation to a standard score or percentile rank or the like.
Affect	A subjective feeling or emotional tone often accompanied by bodily expressions noticeable to others is called affect.
Normative	The term normative is used to describe the effects of those structures of culture which regulate the function of social activity.
Developmental level	An individual's current state of physical, emotional, and intellectual development is called the developmental level.
Frequency distribution	In statistics, a frequency distribution is a list of the values that a variable takes in a sample. It is usually a list, ordered by quantity, showing the number of times each value appears.
Learning	Learning is a relatively permanent change in behavior that results from experience. Thus, to attribute a behavioral change to learning, the change must be relatively permanent and must result from experience.
Baseline	Measure of a particular behavior or process taken before the introduction of the independent variable or treatment is called the baseline.
Histogram	In statistics, a histogram is a graphical display of tabulated frequencies. It is the graphical version of a table which shows what proportion of cases fall into each of several or many specified categories. The categories are usually specified as nonoverlapping intervals of some variable.
Frequency polygon	A graphic representation of a frequency distribution that connects the points that show the frequencies with which scores appear, thereby creating a multisided geometric figure is a frequency polygon.
Normal curve	Normal curve refers to graphic presentation of a normal distribution, which shows a characteristic bell shape.
Personality	Personality refers to the pattern of enduring characteristics that differentiates a person, the patterns of behaviors that make each individual unique.
Trait	An enduring personality characteristic that tends to lead to certain behaviors is called a trait. The term trait also means a genetically inherited feature of an organism.
Central tendency	In statistics, central tendency is an average of a set of measurements, the word average being variously construed as mean, median, or other measure of location, depending on the context. Central tendency is a descriptive statistic analogous to center of mass in physical terms.
Median	The median is a number that separates the higher half of a sample, a population, or a probability distribution from the lower half. It is the middle value in a distribution, above and below which lie an equal number of values.

Variability	Statistically, variability refers to how much the scores in a distribution spread out, away from the mean.
Clustering	Clustering is a technique used to enhance the memory by organization of conceptually-related categories.
Standard deviation	In probability and statistics, the standard deviation is the most commonly used measure of statistical dispersion. Simply put, it measures how spread out the values in a data set are.
Population	Population refers to all members of a well-defined group of organisms, events, or things.
Individual differences	Individual differences psychology studies the ways in which individual people differ in their behavior. This is distinguished from other aspects of psychology in that although psychology is ostensibly a study of individuals, modern psychologists invariably study groups.
Variance	The degree to which scores differ among individuals in a distribution of scores is the variance.
Normal distribution	A normal distribution is a symmetrical distribution of scores that is assumed to reflect chance fluctuations; approximately 68% of cases lie within a single standard deviation of the mean.
Developmental norms	The average age at which individuals display various behaviors and abilities are called developmental norms.
Mental age	The mental age refers to the accumulated months of credit that a person earns on the Stanford-Binet Intelligence Scale.
Adaptation	Adaptation is a lowering of sensitivity to a stimulus following prolonged exposure to that stimulus. Behavioral adaptations are special ways a particular organism behaves to survive in its natural habitat.
Achievement test	A test designed to determine a person's level of knowledge in a given subject area is referred to as an achievement test.
Intelligence test	An intelligence test is a standardized means of assessing a person's current mental ability, for example, the Stanford-Binet test and the Wechsler Adult Intelligence Scale.
Pupil	In the eye, the pupil is the opening in the middle of the iris. It appears black because most of the light entering it is absorbed by the tissues inside the eye. The size of the pupil is controlled by involuntary contraction and dilation of the iris, in order to regulate the intensity of light entering the eye. This is known as the pupillary reflex.
Concept formation	Concept formation refers to the process of classifying information into meaningful categories based on like or unlike properties.
Discrimination	In Learning theory, discrimination refers the ability to distinguish between a conditioned stimulus and other stimuli. It can be brought about by extensive training or differential reinforcement. In social terms, it is the denial of privileges to a person or a group on the basis of prejudice.
Empirical	Empirical means the use of working hypotheses which are capable of being disproved using observation or experiment.
Theories	Theories are logically self-consistent models or frameworks describing the behavior of a certain natural or social phenomenon. They are broad explanations and predictions concerning phenomena of interest.
Infancy	The developmental period that extends from birth to 18 or 24 months is called infancy.
Piaget	Piaget argued that young children's answers were qualitatively different than older children rather than quantitative. There are two major aspects to his theory: the process of coming to

Go to **Cram101.com** for the Practice Tests for this Chapter.

know and the stages we move through as we gradually acquire this ability.

Stages	Stages represent relatively discrete periods of time in which functioning is qualitatively different from functioning at other periods.
Conservation	Conservation refers to the recognition that basic properties of substances such as weight and mass remain the same even when transformations merely alter their appearance.
Rods	Rods are cylindrical shaped photoreceptors that are sensitive to the intensity of light. Rods require less light to function than cone cells, and therefore are the primary source of visual information at night.
Child development	Scientific study of the processes of change from conception through adolescence is called child development.
Guttman scale	The Guttman scale is a comparative scaling technique. It proposes that those who agree with a more extreme test item will also agree with all less extreme items that preceded it.
Ordinal scale	An ordinal scale defines a total preorder of objects; using ranks instead of actual numbers.
Standardized test	An oral or written assessment for which an individual receives a score indicating how the individual reponded relative to a previously tested large sample of others is referred to as a standardized test.
Chronological age	Chronological age refers to the number of years that have elapsed since a person's birth.
Quantitative	A quantitative property is one that exists in a range of magnitudes, and can therefore be measured. Measurements of any particular quantitative property are expressed as as a specific quantity, referred to as a unit, multiplied by a number.
Percentile score	A figure that indicates the percentage of people who score below the score the individual of interest has obtained, is called the percentile score.
Piagetian approach	A Piagetian approach is the study of cognitive development where there are a distinct sequence of qualitative critical stages that are met biologically, experientially, and cognitively.
Percentile rank	The percentile rank of a score is the percentage of scores in its frequency distribution which are lower.
Intelligence quotient	An intelligence quotient is a score derived from a set of standardized tests that were developed with the purpose of measuring a person's cognitive abilities ("intelligence") in relation to their age group.
Psychometric	Psychometric study is concerned with the theory and technique of psychological measurement, which includes the measurement of knowledge, abilities, attitudes, and personality traits. The field is primarily concerned with the study of differences between individuals
Construct	A generalized concept, such as anxiety or gravity, is a construct.
Stanford-Binet	Terman released the "Stanford Revision of the Binet-Simon Scale" or the Stanford-Binet for short. Using validation experiments, he removed several of the Binet-Simon test items and added new ones. In 1985 it was revised to analyze an individual's responses in four content areas: verbal reasoning, quantitative reasoning, abstract reasoning, and short-term memory.
Clinician	A health professional authorized to provide services to people suffering from one or more pathologies is a clinician.
Random sample	A sample drawn so that each member of a population has an equal chance of being selected to participate is referred to as a random sample.

Test norms	Test norms are standards that provide information about where a score on a psychological test ranks in relation to other scores on that test .
Socioeconomic	Socioeconomic pertains to the study of the social and economic impacts of any product or service offering, market intervention or other activity on an economy as a whole and on the companies, organization and individuals who are its main economic actors.
Attention	Attention is the cognitive process of selectively concentrating on one thing while ignoring other things. Psychologists have labeled three types of attention: sustained attention, selective attention, and divided attention.
Anchor	An anchor is a sample of work or performance used to set the specific performance standard for a rubric level .
Reading comprehension	Reading comprehension can be defined as the level of understanding of a passage or text. For normal reading rates (around 200-220 words per minute) an acceptable level of comprehension is above 75%.
Variable	A variable refers to a measurable factor, characteristic, or attribute of an individual or a system.
Scholastic Assessment Test	The Scholastic Assessment Test is a standardized test frequently used by colleges and universities to aid in the selection of incoming students.
Psychological testing	Psychological testing is a field characterized by the use of small samples of behavior in order to infer larger generalizations about a given individual. The technical term for psychological testing is psychometrics.
Acquisition	Acquisition is the process of adapting to the environment, learning or becoming conditioned. In classical conditoning terms, it is the initial learning of the stimulus response link, which involves a neutral stimulus being associated with a unconditioned stimulus and becoming a conditioned stimulus.
All-or-none	All-or-none indicates a situation in which there are two possibilities (a binary choice set), one of which is 100% and one of which is 0%. It is a phrase commonly used to describe action potentials of neurons, which, if they fire at all, propagate from the beginning to the end of the axonal process.
Hypothesis	A specific statement about behavior or mental processes that is testable through research is a hypothesis.
Critical thinking	Critical thinking is a mental process of analyzing or evaluating information, particularly statements or propositions that are offered as true.
Norm-referenced testing	Norm-referenced testing is taking the test-taker's score and comparing it to the test's norms which are derived from standardized samples.
Aptitude test	A test designed to predict a person's ability in a particular area or line of work is called an aptitude test.
Reasoning	Reasoning is the act of using reason to derive a conclusion from certain premises. There are two main methods to reach a conclusion,deductive reasoning and inductive reasoning.

Variable	A variable refers to a measurable factor, characteristic, or attribute of an individual or a system.
Reliability	Reliability means the extent to which a test produces a consistent , reproducible score .
Individual differences	Individual differences psychology studies the ways in which individual people differ in their behavior. This is distinguished from other aspects of psychology in that although psychology is ostensibly a study of individuals, modern psychologists invariably study groups.
Test reliability	Test Reliability is the extent to which a test is repeatable and yields consistent scores.
Variance	The degree to which scores differ among individuals in a distribution of scores is the variance.
Trait	An enduring personality characteristic that tends to lead to certain behaviors is called a trait. The term trait also means a genetically inherited feature of an organism.
Variability	Statistically, variability refers to how much the scores in a distribution spread out, away from the mean.
Personality	Personality refers to the pattern of enduring characteristics that differentiates a person, the patterns of behaviors that make each individual unique.
Correlation coefficient	Correlation coefficient refers to a number from +1.00 to -1.00 that expresses the direction and extent of the relationship between two variables. The closer to 1, the stronger the relationship. The sign, + or -, indicates the direction.
Correlation	A statistical technique for determining the degree of association between two or more variables is referred to as correlation.
Positive correlation	A relationship between two variables in which both vary in the same direction is called a positive correlation.
Negative correlation	A negative correlation refers to a relationship between two variables in which one variable increases as the other decreases.
Raw score	A raw score is an original datum that has not been transformed – for example, the original result obtained by a student on a test (i.e., the number of correctly answered items) as opposed to that score after transformation to a standard score or percentile rank or the like.
Statistical significance	The condition that exists when the probability that the observed findings are due to chance is very low is called statistical significance.
Standard deviation	In probability and statistics, the standard deviation is the most commonly used measure of statistical dispersion. Simply put, it measures how spread out the values in a data set are.
Population	Population refers to all members of a well-defined group of organisms, events, or things.
Significance test	A test to see whether the differences between sets of data could have occurred by chance or if they are real is a significance test.
Attention	Attention is the cognitive process of selectively concentrating on one thing while ignoring other things. Psychologists have labeled three types of attention: sustained attention, selective attention, and divided attention.
Psychometric	Psychometric study is concerned with the theory and technique of psychological measurement, which includes the measurement of knowledge, abilities, attitudes, and personality traits. The field is primarily concerned with the study of differences between individuals
Scatter diagram	A scatter diagram is a graph used in statistics to visually display and compare two or more sets of related quantitative, or numerical, data by displaying only finitely many points,

Go to **Cram101.com** for the Practice Tests for this Chapter.

each having a coordinate on a horizontal and a vertical axis.

Intelligence test	An intelligence test is a standardized means of assessing a person's current mental ability, for example, the Stanford-Binet test and the Wechsler Adult Intelligence Scale.
Affect	A subjective feeling or emotional tone often accompanied by bodily expressions noticeable to others is called affect.
Stanford-Binet	Terman released the "Stanford Revision of the Binet-Simon Scale" or the Stanford-Binet for short. Using validation experiments, he removed several of the Binet-Simon test items and added new ones. In 1985 it was revised to analyze an individual's responses in four content areas: verbal reasoning, quantitative reasoning, abstract reasoning, and short-term memory.
Psychological test	Psychological test refers to a standardized measure of a sample of a person's behavior.
Discrimination	In Learning theory, discrimination refers the ability to distinguish between a conditioned stimulus and other stimuli. It can be brought about by extensive training or differential reinforcement. In social terms, it is the denial of privileges to a person or a group on the basis of prejudice.
Test-retest reliability	The consistency of a measure when it is repeated over time is called test-retest reliability. It involves administering the test to the same group of people at least twice. The first set of scores is correlated with the second set of scores. Correlations range between 0 (low reliability) and 1 (high reliability).
Alternate-form reliability	Alternate-Form Reliability is a statistical technique used to estimate the reliability or internal consistency of a psychological or educational test. By administering two equivalent yet alternate forms of the test to a group of subjects, their scores on the two forms can be compared to each other. When the scores are similar (measured as correlation), the alternate form reliability is high.
Motivation	In psychology, motivation is the driving force (desire) behind all actions of an organism.
Homogeneous	In biology homogeneous has a meaning similar to its meaning in mathematics. Generally it means "the same" or "of the same quality or general property".
Heterogeneous	A heterogeneous compound, mixture, or other such object is one that consists of many different items, which are often not easily sorted or separated, though they are clearly distinct.
Reasoning	Reasoning is the act of using reason to derive a conclusion from certain premises. There are two main methods to reach a conclusion, deductive reasoning and inductive reasoning.
Construct	A generalized concept, such as anxiety or gravity, is a construct.
Cronbach	Cronbach is most famous for the development of Cronbach's alpha, a method for determining the reliability of educational and psychological tests. His work on test reliability reached an acme with the creation of generalizability theory, a statistical model for identifying and quantifying the sources of measurement error.
All-or-none	All-or-none indicates a situation in which there are two possibilities (a binary choice set), one of which is 100% and one of which is 0%. It is a phrase commonly used to describe action potentials of neurons, which, if they fire at all, propagate from the beginning to the end of the axonal process.
Personality inventory	A self-report questionnaire by which an examinee indicates whether statements assessing habitual tendencies apply to him or her is referred to as a personality inventory.
Projective test	A projective test is a personality test designed to let a person respond to ambiguous stimuli, presumably revealing hidden emotions and internal conflicts. This is different from

an "objective test" in which responses are analyzed according to a universal standard rather than an individual psychiatrist's judgement.

Creativity	Creativity is the ability to think about something in novel and unusual ways and come up with unique solutions to problems. It involves divergent thinking, having many solutions or views to a problem.
Random sample	A sample drawn so that each member of a population has an equal chance of being selected to participate is referred to as a random sample.
Generalizability	The ability to extend a set of findings observed in one piece of research to other situations and groups is called generalizability.
Fisher	Fisher was a eugenicist, evolutionary biologist, geneticist and statistician. He has been described as "The greatest of Darwin's successors", and a genius who almost single-handedly created the foundations for modern statistical science inventing the techniques of maximum likelihood and analysis of variance.
Power test	A test without a time limit is referred to as a power test.
Primary mental abilities	According to Thurstone, the basic abilities that make up intelligence are called primary mental abilities.
Aptitude test	A test designed to predict a person's ability in a particular area or line of work is called an aptitude test.
Statistics	Statistics is a type of data analysis which practice includes the planning, summarizing, and interpreting of observations of a system possibly followed by predicting or forecasting of future events based on a mathematical model of the system being observed.
Statistic	A statistic is an observable random variable of a sample.
Standard error of measurement	The estimate of the 'error' associated with the test-taker's obtained score when compared with their hypothetical 'true' score is standard error of measurement. The standard error of measurement, which varies from test to test, should be given in the test manual.
Normal curve	Normal curve refers to graphic presentation of a normal distribution, which shows a characteristic bell shape.
Counselor	A counselor is a mental health professional who specializes in helping people with problems not involving serious mental disorders.

Validity	The extent to which a test measures what it is intended to measure is called validity.
Empirical	Empirical means the use of working hypotheses which are capable of being disproved using observation or experiment.
Trait	An enduring personality characteristic that tends to lead to certain behaviors is called a trait. The term trait also means a genetically inherited feature of an organism.
Experimental hypothesis	The experimental hypothesis is what the investigator assumes will happen in a scientific investigation if certain conditions are met or particular variables are manipulated.
Hypothesis	A specific statement about behavior or mental processes that is testable through research is a hypothesis.
Construct	A generalized concept, such as anxiety or gravity, is a construct.
Variable	A variable refers to a measurable factor, characteristic, or attribute of an individual or a system.
Construct validity	The extent to which there is evidence that a test measures a particular hypothetical construct is referred to as construct validity.
Cronbach	Cronbach is most famous for the development of Cronbach's alpha, a method for determining the reliability of educational and psychological tests. His work on test reliability reached an acme with the creation of generalizability theory, a statistical model for identifying and quantifying the sources of measurement error.
Content validity	The degree to which the content of a test is representative of the domain it's supposed to cover is referred to as its content validity.
Achievement test	A test designed to determine a person's level of knowledge in a given subject area is referred to as an achievement test.
Personality test	A personality test aims to describe aspects of a person's character that remain stable across situations.
Personality	Personality refers to the pattern of enduring characteristics that differentiates a person, the patterns of behaviors that make each individual unique.
Individual differences	Individual differences psychology studies the ways in which individual people differ in their behavior. This is distinguished from other aspects of psychology in that although psychology is ostensibly a study of individuals, modern psychologists invariably study groups.
Reasoning	Reasoning is the act of using reason to derive a conclusion from certain premises. There are two main methods to reach a conclusion, deductive reasoning and inductive reasoning.
Face validity	Condition of testing in which test items appear plausible for their intended purposes is called face validity.
Affect	A subjective feeling or emotional tone often accompanied by bodily expressions noticeable to others is called affect.
Attention	Attention is the cognitive process of selectively concentrating on one thing while ignoring other things. Psychologists have labeled three types of attention: sustained attention, selective attention, and divided attention.
Attitude	An enduring mental representation of a person, place, or thing that evokes an emotional response and related behavior is called attitude.
Questionnaire	A self-report method of data collection or clinical assessment method in which the individual being studied checks off items on a printed list, answers multiple-choice questions, or writes out answers to essay questions aimed at producing a selfdescription is called

Go to **Cram101.com** for the Practice Tests for this Chapter.

	questionnaire.
Feedback	Feedback refers to information returned to a person about the effects a response has had.
Reliability	Reliability means the extent to which a test produces a consistent , reproducible score .
Quantitative	A quantitative property is one that exists in a range of magnitudes, and can therefore be measured. Measurements of any particular quantitative property are expressed as as a specific quantity, referred to as a unit, multiplied by a number.
Predictive validity	Predictive validity refers to the relation between test scores and the student 's future performance .
Criterion contamination	The extent to which an actual criterion assesses something other than the theoretical criterion is referred to as criterion contamination.
Intelligence test	An intelligence test is a standardized means of assessing a person's current mental ability, for example, the Stanford-Binet test and the Wechsler Adult Intelligence Scale.
Aptitude test	A test designed to predict a person's ability in a particular area or line of work is called an aptitude test.
Attitude scale	A multiple-item questionnaire designed to measure a person's attitude toward some object is called an attitude scale.
Adaptation	Adaptation is a lowering of sensitivity to a stimulus following prolonged exposure to that stimulus. Behavioral adaptations are special ways a particular organism behaves to survive in its natural habitat.
Correlation	A statistical technique for determining the degree of association between two or more variables is referred to as correlation.
Counselor	A counselor is a mental health professional who specializes in helping people with problems not involving serious mental disorders.
Stanford-Binet	Terman released the "Stanford Revision of the Binet-Simon Scale" or the Stanford-Binet for short. Using validation experiments, he removed several of the Binet-Simon test items and added new ones. In 1985 it was revised to analyze an individual's responses in four content areas: verbal reasoning, quantitative reasoning, abstract reasoning, and short-term memory.
Validity generalization	A principle that states that if a predictor is a valid indicator of a criterion in one setting, it will be valid in another similar setting is the validity generalization.
Generalization	In conditioning, the tendency for a conditioned response to be evoked by stimuli that are similar to the stimulus to which the response was conditioned is a generalization. The greater the similarity among the stimuli, the greater the probability of generalization.
Test battery	A group of tests and interviews given to the same individual is a test battery.
Generalizability	The ability to extend a set of findings observed in one piece of research to other situations and groups is called generalizability.
Variability	Statistically, variability refers to how much the scores in a distribution spread out, away from the mean.
Standardized test	An oral or written assessment for which an individual receives a score indicating how the individual reponded relative to a previously tested large sample of others is referred to as a standardized test.
Variance	The degree to which scores differ among individuals in a distribution of scores is the variance.
Cognitive skills	Cognitive skills such as reasoning, attention, and memory can be advanced and sustained

Go to **Cram101.com** for the Practice Tests for this Chapter.

through practice and training.

Meta-analysis	In statistics, a meta-analysis combines the results of several studies that address a set of related research hypotheses.
Control group	A group that does not receive the treatment effect in an experiment is referred to as the control group or sometimes as the comparison group.
Survey	A method of scientific investigation in which a large sample of people answer questions about their attitudes or behavior is referred to as a survey.
Effect size	An effect size is the strength or magnitude of the difference between two sets of data or, in outcome studies, between two time points for the same population. (The degree to which the null hypothesis is false).
Psychological test	Psychological test refers to a standardized measure of a sample of a person's behavior.
Ordinal scale	An ordinal scale defines a total preorder of objects; using ranks instead of actual numbers.
Invariance	Invariance is the property of perception whereby simple geometrical objects are recognized independent of rotation, translation, and scale, as well as several other variations such as elastic deformations, different lighting, and different component features.
Factor analysis	Factor analysis is a statistical technique that originated in psychometrics. The objective is to explain the most of the variability among a number of observable random variables in terms of a smaller number of unobservable random variables called factors.
Common traits	Common traits, according to Allport, are personality characteristics that are shared by most members of a particular culture or grouping.
Achievement motivation	The psychological need in humans for success is called achievement motivation.
Motivation	In psychology, motivation is the driving force (desire) behind all actions of an organism.
Anxiety	Anxiety is a complex combination of the feeling of fear, apprehension and worry often accompanied by physical sensations such as palpitations, chest pain and/or shortness of breath.
Acquisition	Acquisition is the process of adapting to the environment, learning or becoming conditioned. In classical conditoning terms, it is the initial learning of the stimulus response link, which involves a neutral stimulus being associated with a unconditioned stimulus and becoming a conditioned stimulus.
Learning	Learning is a relatively permanent change in behavior that results from experience. Thus, to attribute a behavioral change to learning, the change must be relatively permanent and must result from experience.
Statistics	Statistics is a type of data analysis which practice includes the planning, summarizing, and interpreting of observations of a system possibly followed by predicting or forecasting of future events based on a mathematical model of the system being observed.
Causation	Causation concerns the time order relationship between two or more objects such that if a specific antecendent condition occurs the same consequent must always follow.
Statistic	A statistic is an observable random variable of a sample.
Modeling	A type of behavior learned through observation of others demonstrating the same behavior is modeling.
Independent	A condition in a scientific study that is manipulated (assigned different values by a

Go to **Cram101.com** for the Practice Tests for this Chapter.
And, **NEVER** highlight a book again!

variable	researcher) so that the effects of the manipulation may be observed is called an independent variable.
Regression equation	A regression equation refers to a mathematical relationship where one variable is predictable from another.
Regression	Return to a form of behavior characteristic of an earlier stage of development is called regression.
Goodness of Fit	With respect to care giving, the degree to which parents and children have compatible temperaments is called goodness of fit.
Educational psychology	Educational psychology is the study of how children and adults learn, the effectiveness of various educational strategies and tactics, and how schools function as organizations.
Cognitive psychology	Cognitive psychology is the psychological science which studies the mental processes that are hypothesised to underlie behavior. This covers a broad range of research domains, examining questions about the workings of memory, attention, perception, knowledge representation, reasoning, creativity and problem solving.
Experimental psychology	Experimental psychology is an approach to psychology that treats it as one of the natural sciences, and therefore assumes that it is susceptible to the experimental method.
Information processing	Information processing is an approach to the goal of understanding human thinking. The essence of the approach is to see cognition as being essentially computational in nature, with mind being the software and the brain being the hardware.
Psychometric	Psychometric study is concerned with the theory and technique of psychological measurement, which includes the measurement of knowledge, abilities, attitudes, and personality traits. The field is primarily concerned with the study of differences between individuals
Task analysis	The procedure of identifying the component elements of a behavior chain is called task analysis.
Metacognition	Metacognition refers to thinking about cognition (memory, perception, calculation, association, etc.) itself. Metacognition can be divided into two types of knowledge: explicit, conscious, factual knowledge; and implicit, unconscious, procedural knowledge.
Sternberg	Sternberg proposed the triarchic theory of intelligence: componential, experiential, and practical. His notion of general intelligence or the g-factor, is a composite of intelligence scores across multiple modalities.
Nomothetic	Nomothetic measures are contrasted to ipsative or idiothetic measures, where nomothetic measures are measures that can be taken directly by an outside observer, such as weight or how many times a particular behavior occurs, and ipsative measures are self-reports such as a rank-ordered list of preferences.
Decomposition	An arithmetic type of strategy in which children transform the original problem into two or more simpler problems is called decomposition.
Information-processing approach	Information-processing approach emphasizes that individuals act on information, monitor it, and strategize about it--contrary to strict behaviorists. Central to information processing are the processes of memory and thinking. The computer serves as a metaphor whereby the brain is the hardware and behavior is the software.
Heuristic	A heuristic is a simple, efficient rule of thumb proposed to explain how people make decisions, come to judgments and solve problems, typically when facing complex problems or incomplete information. These rules work well under most circumstances, but in certain cases lead to systematic cognitive biases.
Population	Population refers to all members of a well-defined group of organisms, events, or things.

Go to **Cram101.com** for the Practice Tests for this Chapter.

Criterion-related validity	Test validity that is estimated by correlating subjects' scores on a test with their scores on an independent criterion of the variable assessed by the test is referred to as criterion-related validity.
Stages	Stages represent relatively discrete periods of time in which functioning is qualitatively different from functioning at other periods.
Normative	The term normative is used to describe the effects of those structures of culture which regulate the function of social activity.
Norms	In testing, standards of test performance that permit the comparison of one person's score on the test to the scores of others who have taken the same test are referred to as norms.
Society	The social sciences use the term society to mean a group of people that form a semi-closed (or semi-open) social system, in which most interactions are with other individuals belonging to the group.

Go to **Cram101.com** for the Practice Tests for this Chapter.

Validity	The extent to which a test measures what it is intended to measure is called validity.
Construct validity	The extent to which there is evidence that a test measures a particular hypothetical construct is referred to as construct validity.
Construct	A generalized concept, such as anxiety or gravity, is a construct.
Inference	Inference is the act or process of drawing a conclusion based solely on what one already knows.
Correlation	A statistical technique for determining the degree of association between two or more variables is referred to as correlation.
Statistics	Statistics is a type of data analysis which practice includes the planning, summarizing, and interpreting of observations of a system possibly followed by predicting or forecasting of future events based on a mathematical model of the system being observed.
Statistic	A statistic is an observable random variable of a sample.
Reliability	Reliability means the extent to which a test produces a consistent , reproducible score .
Population	Population refers to all members of a well-defined group of organisms, events, or things.
Generalizability	The ability to extend a set of findings observed in one piece of research to other situations and groups is called generalizability.
Homogeneous	In biology homogeneous has a meaning similar to its meaning in mathematics. Generally it means "the same" or "of the same quality or general property".
Correlation coefficient	Correlation coefficient refers to a number from +1.00 to -1.00 that expresses the direction and extent of the relationship between two variables. The closer to 1, the stronger the relationship. The sign, + or -, indicates the direction.
Reading comprehension	Reading comprehension can be defined as the level of understanding of a passage or text. For normal reading rates (around 200-220 words per minute) an acceptable level of comprehension is above 75%.
Scatter diagram	A scatter diagram is a graph used in statistics to visually display and compare two or more sets of related quantitative, or numerical, data by displaying only finitely many points, each having a coordinate on a horizontal and a vertical axis.
Variability	Statistically, variability refers to how much the scores in a distribution spread out, away from the mean.
Psychological test	Psychological test refers to a standardized measure of a sample of a person's behavior.
Affect	A subjective feeling or emotional tone often accompanied by bodily expressions noticeable to others is called affect.
Attention	Attention is the cognitive process of selectively concentrating on one thing while ignoring other things. Psychologists have labeled three types of attention: sustained attention, selective attention, and divided attention.
Cronbach	Cronbach is most famous for the development of Cronbach's alpha, a method for determining the reliability of educational and psychological tests. His work on test reliability reached an acme with the creation of generalizability theory, a statistical model for identifying and quantifying the sources of measurement error.
Psychological testing	Psychological testing is a field characterized by the use of small samples of behavior in order to infer larger generalizations about a given individual. The technical term for psychological testing is psychometrics.

Go to **Cram101.com** for the Practice Tests for this Chapter.

41

Clinical psychology	Clinical psychology is involved in the diagnosis, assessment, and treatment of patients with mental or behavioral disorders, and conducts research in these various areas.
Brain	The brain controls and coordinates most movement, behavior and homeostatic body functions such as heartbeat, blood pressure, fluid balance and body temperature. Functions of the brain are responsible for cognition, emotion, memory, motor learning and other sorts of learning. The brain is primarily made up of two types of cells: glia and neurons.
False positive	A false positive, also called a Type I error, exists when a test incorrectly reports that it has found a result where none really exists.
False negative	A false negative, also called a Type II error or miss, exists when a test incorrectly reports that a result was not detected, when it was really present.
Aptitude test	A test designed to predict a person's ability in a particular area or line of work is called an aptitude test.
Random selection	Choosing a sample so that each member of the population has an equal chance of being included in the sample is called random selection.
Schematic representation	The representation of objects in terms of real or potential interactions with other objects is called a schematic representation.
Psychological disorder	Mental processes and/or behavior patterns that cause emotional distress and/or substantial impairment in functioning is a psychological disorder.
Stages	Stages represent relatively discrete periods of time in which functioning is qualitatively different from functioning at other periods.
Moderator variable	A variable that affects the relation between two other variables is called the moderator variable.
Variable	A variable refers to a measurable factor, characteristic, or attribute of an individual or a system.
Psychometric	Psychometric study is concerned with the theory and technique of psychological measurement, which includes the measurement of knowledge, abilities, attitudes, and personality traits. The field is primarily concerned with the study of differences between individuals
Variance	The degree to which scores differ among individuals in a distribution of scores is the variance.
Heuristic	A heuristic is a simple, efficient rule of thumb proposed to explain how people make decisions, come to judgments and solve problems, typically when facing complex problems or incomplete information. These rules work well under most circumstances, but in certain cases lead to systematic cognitive biases.
Trait	An enduring personality characteristic that tends to lead to certain behaviors is called a trait. The term trait also means a genetically inherited feature of an organism.
Test battery	A group of tests and interviews given to the same individual is a test battery.
Regression equation	A regression equation refers to a mathematical relationship where one variable is predictable from another.
Multiple regression	A multiple regression is a linear regression with more than one covariate (predictor variable). It can be viewed as a simple case of canonical correlation.
Regression	Return to a form of behavior characteristic of an earlier stage of development is called regression.
Reasoning	Reasoning is the act of using reason to derive a conclusion from certain premises. There are

	two main methods to reach a conclusion,deductive reasoning and inductive reasoning.
Empirical	Empirical means the use of working hypotheses which are capable of being disproved using observation or experiment.
Predictive validity	Predictive validity refers to the relation between test scores and the student 's future performance .
Clinical assessment	A clinical assessment is a systematic evaluation and measurement of psychological, biological, and social factors in a person presenting with a possible psychological disorder.
Individual differences	Individual differences psychology studies the ways in which individual people differ in their behavior. This is distinguished from other aspects of psychology in that although psychology is ostensibly a study of individuals, modern psychologists invariably study groups.
Negative correlation	A negative correlation refers to a relationship between two variables in which one variable increases as the other decreases.
Intelligence test	An intelligence test is a standardized means of assessing a person's current mental ability, for example, the Stanford-Binet test and the Wechsler Adult Intelligence Scale.
Syndrome	The term syndrome is the association of several clinically recognizable features, signs, symptoms, phenomena or characteristics which often occur together, so that the presence of one feature indicates the presence of the others.
Standard deviation	In probability and statistics, the standard deviation is the most commonly used measure of statistical dispersion. Simply put, it measures how spread out the values in a data set are.
Content validity	The degree to which the content of a test is representative of the domain it's supposed to cover is referred to as its content validity.
Subculture	As understood in sociology, anthropology and cultural studies, a subculture is a set of people with a distinct set of behavior and beliefs that differentiate them from a larger culture of which they are a part.
Statistical significance	The condition that exists when the probability that the observed findings are due to chance is very low is called statistical significance.
Achievement test	A test designed to determine a person's level of knowledge in a given subject area is referred to as an achievement test.
Ethnic group	An ethnic group is a culture or subculture whose members are readily distinguishable by outsiders based on traits originating from a common racial, national, linguistic, or religious source. Members of an ethnic group are often presumed to be culturally or biologically similar, although this is not in fact necessarily the case.
Survey	A method of scientific investigation in which a large sample of people answer questions about their attitudes or behavior is referred to as a survey.
Socioeconomic	Socioeconomic pertains to the study of the social and economic impacts of any product or service offering, market intervention or other activity on an economy as a whole and on the companies, organization and individuals who are its main economic actors.
Self-concept	Self-concept refers to domain-specific evaluations of the self where a domain may be academics, athletics, etc.
Stereotype	A stereotype is considered to be a group concept, held by one social group about another.They are often used in a negative or prejudicial sense and are frequently used to justify certain discriminatory behaviors. This allows powerful social groups to legitimize and protect their dominant position
Attitude	An enduring mental representation of a person, place, or thing that evokes an emotional

response and related behavior is called attitude.

Personality trait   According to the Diagnostic and Statistical Manual of the American Psychiatric Association, a personality trait is a "prominent aspect of personality that is exhibited in a wide range of important social and personal contexts. ...".

Personality   Personality refers to the pattern of enduring characteristics that differentiates a person, the patterns of behaviors that make each individual unique.

Motivation   In psychology, motivation is the driving force (desire) behind all actions of an organism.

Discrimination	In Learning theory, discrimination refers the ability to distinguish between a conditioned stimulus and other stimuli. It can be brought about by extensive training or differential reinforcement. In social terms, it is the denial of privileges to a person or a group on the basis of prejudice.
Quantitative	A quantitative property is one that exists in a range of magnitudes, and can therefore be measured. Measurements of any particular quantitative property are expressed as as a specific quantity, referred to as a unit, multiplied by a number.
Reliability	Reliability means the extent to which a test produces a consistent , reproducible score .
Validity	The extent to which a test measures what it is intended to measure is called validity.
Random selection	Choosing a sample so that each member of the population has an equal chance of being included in the sample is called random selection.
Individual differences	Individual differences psychology studies the ways in which individual people differ in their behavior. This is distinguished from other aspects of psychology in that although psychology is ostensibly a study of individuals, modern psychologists invariably study groups.
Variability	Statistically, variability refers to how much the scores in a distribution spread out, away from the mean.
Affect	A subjective feeling or emotional tone often accompanied by bodily expressions noticeable to others is called affect.
Homogeneous	In biology homogeneous has a meaning similar to its meaning in mathematics. Generally it means "the same" or "of the same quality or general property".
Correlation	A statistical technique for determining the degree of association between two or more variables is referred to as correlation.
Ordinal scale	An ordinal scale defines a total preorder of objects; using ranks instead of actual numbers.
Percentile score	A figure that indicates the percentage of people who score below the score the individual of interest has obtained, is called the percentile score.
Normal distribution	A normal distribution is a symmetrical distribution of scores that is assumed to reflect chance fluctuations; approximately 68% of cases lie within a single standard deviation of the mean.
Normal curve	Normal curve refers to graphic presentation of a normal distribution, which shows a characteristic bell shape.
Achievement test	A test designed to determine a person's level of knowledge in a given subject area is referred to as an achievement test.
Thurstone	Thurstone was a pioneer in the field of psychometrics. His work in factor analysis led him to formulate a model of intelligence center around "Primary Mental Abilities", which were independent group factors of intelligence that different individuals possessed in varying degrees.
Anchor	An anchor is a sample of work or performance used to set the specific performance standard for a rubric level .
Population	Population refers to all members of a well-defined group of organisms, events, or things.
Skewness	In probability theory and statistics, skewness is a measure of the asymmetry of the probability distribution of a real-valued random variable. Roughly speaking, a distribution has positive skew (right-skewed) if the higher tail is longer and negative skew (left-skewed) if the lower tail is longer (confusing the two is a common error).

Go to **Cram101.com** for the Practice Tests for this Chapter.

Inference	Inference is the act or process of drawing a conclusion based solely on what one already knows.
Psychological test	Psychological test refers to a standardized measure of a sample of a person's behavior.
Learning	Learning is a relatively permanent change in behavior that results from experience. Thus, to attribute a behavioral change to learning, the change must be relatively permanent and must result from experience.
Clustering	Clustering is a technique used to enhance the memory by organization of conceptually-related categories.
A priori	The term A Priori is considered to mean propositional knowledge that can be had without, or "prior to", experience.
Syndrome	The term syndrome is the association of several clinically recognizable features, signs, symptoms, phenomena or characteristics which often occur together, so that the presence of one feature indicates the presence of the others.
Aptitude test	A test designed to predict a person's ability in a particular area or line of work is called an aptitude test.
Construct	A generalized concept, such as anxiety or gravity, is a construct.
Stages	Stages represent relatively discrete periods of time in which functioning is qualitatively different from functioning at other periods.
Trait	An enduring personality characteristic that tends to lead to certain behaviors is called a trait. The term trait also means a genetically inherited feature of an organism.
External validity	External validity is a term used in scientific research. It signifies the extent to which the results of a study can be applied to circumstances outside the specific setting in which the research was carried out. In other words, it addresses the question "Can this research be applied to 'the real world'?"
Variance	The degree to which scores differ among individuals in a distribution of scores is the variance.
Guilford	Guilford observed that most individuals display a preference for either convergent or divergent thinking. Scientists and engineers typically prefer the former and artists and performers, the latter.
Regression equation	A regression equation refers to a mathematical relationship where one variable is predictable from another.
Regression	Return to a form of behavior characteristic of an earlier stage of development is called regression.
Heterogeneous	A heterogeneous compound, mixture, or other such object is one that consists of many different items, which are often not easily sorted or separated, though they are clearly distinct.
Variable	A variable refers to a measurable factor, characteristic, or attribute of an individual or a system.
Dichotomy	A dichotomy is the division of a proposition into two parts which are both mutually exclusive – i.e. both cannot be simultaneously true – and jointly exhaustive – i.e. they cover the full range of possible outcomes. They are often contrasting and spoken of as "opposites".
Statistics	Statistics is a type of data analysis which practice includes the planning, summarizing, and interpreting of observations of a system possibly followed by predicting or forecasting of

Go to **Cram101.com** for the Practice Tests for this Chapter.
And, **NEVER** highlight a book again!

future events based on a mathematical model of the system being observed.

Statistic	A statistic is an observable random variable of a sample.
Standardized test	An oral or written assessment for which an individual receives a score indicating how the individual reponded relative to a previously tested large sample of others is referred to as a standardized test.
Correlation coefficient	Correlation coefficient refers to a number from +1.00 to -1.00 that expresses the direction and extent of the relationship between two variables. The closer to 1, the stronger the relationship. The sign, + or -, indicates the direction.
Trait theory	According to trait theory, personality can be broken down into a limited number of traits, which are present in each individual to a greater or lesser degree. This approach is highly compatible with the quantitative psychometric approach to personality testing.
Psychometric	Psychometric study is concerned with the theory and technique of psychological measurement, which includes the measurement of knowledge, abilities, attitudes, and personality traits. The field is primarily concerned with the study of differences between individuals
Empirical	Empirical means the use of working hypotheses which are capable of being disproved using observation or experiment.
Invariance	Invariance is the property of perception whereby simple geometrical objects are recognized independent of rotation, translation, and scale, as well as several other variations such as elastic deformations, different lighting, and different component features.
Random sample	A sample drawn so that each member of a population has an equal chance of being selected to participate is referred to as a random sample.
Simulation	A simulation is an imitation of some real device or state of affairs. Simulation attempts to represent certain features of the behavior of a physical or abstract system by the behavior of another system.
Representative sample	Representative sample refers to a sample of participants selected from the larger population in such a way that important subgroups within the population are included in the sample in the same proportions as they are found in the larger population.
Random sampling	The selection of participants in an unbiased manner so that each potential participant has an equal possibility of being selected for the experiment is called random sampling.
Chance variation	Differences between events without any known influence is considered a chance variation.
Rorschach	The Rorschach inkblot test is a method of psychological evaluation. It is a projective test associated with the Freudian school of thought. Psychologists use this test to try to probe the unconscious minds of their patients.
Psychokinesis	The purported ability to mentally alter or influence objects or events is psychokinesis.
Negative correlation	A negative correlation refers to a relationship between two variables in which one variable increases as the other decreases.
Attention	Attention is the cognitive process of selectively concentrating on one thing while ignoring other things. Psychologists have labeled three types of attention: sustained attention, selective attention, and divided attention.
Stereotype	A stereotype is considered to be a group concept, held by one social group about another.They are often used in a negative or prejudicial sense and are frequently used to justify certain discriminatory behaviors. This allows powerful social groups to legitimize and protect their dominant position
Outlier	An outlier is a single observation "far away" from the rest of the data.

Go to **Cram101.com** for the Practice Tests for this Chapter.

53

American Psychological Association	The American Psychological Association is a professional organization representing psychology in the US. The mission statement is to "advance psychology as a science and profession and as a means of promoting health, education , and human welfare".
Cognitive psychology	Cognitive psychology is the psychological science which studies the mental processes that are hypothesised to underlie behavior. This covers a broad range of research domains, examining questions about the workings of memory, attention, perception, knowledge representation, reasoning, creativity and problem solving.
Stimulus	A change in an environmental condition that elicits a response is a stimulus.
Spatial visualization	An aspect of spatial cognition that involves the mental manipulations of visual stimuli, such as performing mental rotation or solving embedded-figures problems is referred to as spatial visualization.
Inductive reasoning	A form of reasoning in which we reason from individual cases or particular facts to a general conclusion is referred to as inductive reasoning. The conclusion can be said to follow with a probability rather than certainty.
Reasoning	Reasoning is the act of using reason to derive a conclusion from certain premises. There are two main methods to reach a conclusion, deductive reasoning and inductive reasoning.
Predictive validity	Predictive validity refers to the relation between test scores and the student 's future performance .
Decomposition	An arithmetic type of strategy in which children transform the original problem into two or more simpler problems is called decomposition.
Nomothetic	Nomothetic measures are contrasted to ipsative or idiothetic measures, where nomothetic measures are measures that can be taken directly by an outside observer, such as weight or how many times a particular behavior occurs, and ipsative measures are self-reports such as a rank-ordered list of preferences.
Overgenerali-ation	Overgeneralization is concluding that all instances of some kind of event will turn out a certain way because one or more in the past did. For instance, a class goes badly one day and I conclude, "I'll never be a good teacher."

Psychological testing	Psychological testing is a field characterized by the use of small samples of behavior in order to infer larger generalizations about a given individual. The technical term for psychological testing is psychometrics.
Survey	A method of scientific investigation in which a large sample of people answer questions about their attitudes or behavior is referred to as a survey.
Intelligence test	An intelligence test is a standardized means of assessing a person's current mental ability, for example, the Stanford-Binet test and the Wechsler Adult Intelligence Scale.
Stanford-Binet	Terman released the "Stanford Revision of the Binet-Simon Scale" or the Stanford-Binet for short. Using validation experiments, he removed several of the Binet-Simon test items and added new ones. In 1985 it was revised to analyze an individual's responses in four content areas: verbal reasoning, quantitative reasoning, abstract reasoning, and short-term memory.
Adaptation	Adaptation is a lowering of sensitivity to a stimulus following prolonged exposure to that stimulus. Behavioral adaptations are special ways a particular organism behaves to survive in its natural habitat.
Terman	Terman revised the Stanford-Binet Intelligence Scale in 1916, commonly used to measure intelligence (or I.Q.) in the United States. William Stern's suggestion that mental age/chronological age times 100 (to get rid of the decimal) be made the "intelligence quotient" or I.Q. This apparent mathematization of the measurement gave it an air of scientific accuracy and detachment which contributed greatly to its acceptance among educators and the broad public.
Psychological test	Psychological test refers to a standardized measure of a sample of a person's behavior.
Socioeconomic	Socioeconomic pertains to the study of the social and economic impacts of any product or service offering, market intervention or other activity on an economy as a whole and on the companies, organization and individuals who are its main economic actors.
Population	Population refers to all members of a well-defined group of organisms, events, or things.
Normative	The term normative is used to describe the effects of those structures of culture which regulate the function of social activity.
Norms	In testing, standards of test performance that permit the comparison of one person's score on the test to the scores of others who have taken the same test are referred to as norms.
Representative sample	Representative sample refers to a sample of participants selected from the larger population in such a way that important subgroups within the population are included in the sample in the same proportions as they are found in the larger population.
Thorndike	Thorndike worked in animal behavior and the learning process leading to the theory of connectionism. Among his most famous contributions were his research on cats escaping from puzzle boxes, and his formulation of the Law of Effect.
Test norms	Test norms are standards that provide information about where a score on a psychological test ranks in relation to other scores on that test .
Individual intelligence test	A test of intelligence designed to be given to a single individual by a trained specialist is an individual intelligence test. Background information supplements the test.
Standardized test	An oral or written assessment for which an individual receives a score indicating how the individual reponded relative to a previously tested large sample of others is referred to as a standardized test.
Clinician	A health professional authorized to provide services to people suffering from one or more

Go to **Cram101.com** for the Practice Tests for this Chapter.

Go to **Cram101.com** for the Practice Tests for this Chapter.
And, **NEVER** highlight a book again!

pathologies is a clinician.

Short-term memory	Short-term memory is that part of memory which stores a limited amount of information for a limited amount of time (roughly 30-45 seconds). The second key concept associated with a short-term memory is that it has a finite capacity.
Quantitative	A quantitative property is one that exists in a range of magnitudes, and can therefore be measured. Measurements of any particular quantitative property are expressed as as a specific quantity, referred to as a unit, multiplied by a number.
Reasoning	Reasoning is the act of using reason to derive a conclusion from certain premises. There are two main methods to reach a conclusion,deductive reasoning and inductive reasoning.
Attention	Attention is the cognitive process of selectively concentrating on one thing while ignoring other things. Psychologists have labeled three types of attention: sustained attention, selective attention, and divided attention.
Chronological age	Chronological age refers to the number of years that have elapsed since a person's birth.
Raw score	A raw score is an original datum that has not been transformed – for example, the original result obtained by a student on a test (i.e., the number of correctly answered items) as opposed to that score after transformation to a standard score or percentile rank or the like.
Ethnic group	An ethnic group is a culture or subculture whose members are readily distinguishable by outsiders based on traits originating from a common racial, national, linguistic, or religious source. Members of an ethnic group are often presumed to be culturally or biologically similar, although this is not in fact necessarily the case.
Socioeconomic Status	A family's socioeconomic status is based on family income, parental education level, parental occupation, and social status in the community. Those with high status often have more success in preparing their children for school because they have access to a wide range of resources.
Test-retest reliability	The consistency of a measure when it is repeated over time is called test-retest reliability. It involves administering the test to the same group of people at least twice. The first set of scores is correlated with the second set of scores. Correlations range between 0 (low reliability) and 1 (high reliability).
Reliability	Reliability means the extent to which a test produces a consistent , reproducible score .
Cohort	A cohort is a group of individuals defined by their date of birth.
Standard error of measurement	The estimate of the 'error' associated with the test-taker's obtained score when compared with their hypothetical 'true' score is standard error of measurement. The standard error of measurement, which varies from test to test, should be given in the test manual.
Wechsler Scales	The Wechsler Scales are two well-known intelligence scales, namely the Wechsler Adult Intelligence Scale and the Wechsler Intelligence Scale for Children.
Statistical significance	The condition that exists when the probability that the observed findings are due to chance is very low is called statistical significance.
Construct	A generalized concept, such as anxiety or gravity, is a construct.
Factor analysis	Factor analysis is a statistical technique that originated in psychometrics. The objective is to explain the most of the variability among a number of observable random variables in terms of a smaller number of unobservable random variables called factors.
Correlation	A statistical technique for determining the degree of association between two or more

Go to **Cram101.com** for the Practice Tests for this Chapter.
And, **NEVER** highlight a book again!

	variables is referred to as correlation.
Median	The median is a number that separates the higher half of a sample, a population, or a probability distribution from the lower half. It is the middle value in a distribution, above and below which lie an equal number of values.
Hypothesis	A specific statement about behavior or mental processes that is testable through research is a hypothesis.
Learning	Learning is a relatively permanent change in behavior that results from experience. Thus, to attribute a behavioral change to learning, the change must be relatively permanent and must result from experience.
Validity	The extent to which a test measures what it is intended to measure is called validity.
Mental retardation	Mental retardation refers to having significantly below-average intellectual functioning and limitations in at least two areas of adaptive functioning. Many categorize retardation as mild, moderate, severe, or profound.
David Wechsler	David Wechsler developed two well-known intelligence scales, namely the Wechsler Adult Intelligence Scale and the Wechsler Intelligence Scale for Children. He held the view that human intelligence is not a single thing, but a mixture of many distinct -- and separately measurable -- human capabilities.
Clinical psychologist	A psychologist, usually with a Ph.D, whose training is in the diagnosis, treatment, or research of psychological and behavioral disorders is a clinical psychologist.
Affect	A subjective feeling or emotional tone often accompanied by bodily expressions noticeable to others is called affect.
Brain	The brain controls and coordinates most movement, behavior and homeostatic body functions such as heartbeat, blood pressure, fluid balance and body temperature. Functions of the brain are responsible for cognition, emotion, memory, motor learning and other sorts of learning. The brain is primarily made up of two types of cells: glia and neurons.
Antecedents	In behavior modification, events that typically precede the target response are called antecedents.
Evolution	Commonly used to refer to gradual change, evolution is the change in the frequency of alleles within a population from one generation to the next. This change may be caused by different mechanisms, including natural selection, genetic drift, or changes in population (gene flow).
Face validity	Condition of testing in which test items appear plausible for their intended purposes is called face validity.
Wechsler Intelligence Scale for Children	The Wechsler Intelligence Scale for Children is an intelligence test that can be completed without reading or writing. It generates an IQ score. It also generates four composite scores; Verbal Comprehension, Perceptual Reasoning, Processing Speed and Working Memory.
Wechsler Adult Intelligence Scale	Wechsler adult intelligence scale is an individual intelligence test for adults that yields separate verbal and performance IQ scores as well as an overall IQ score.
Wechsler adult Intelligence	Wechsler adult Intelligence Scale is a revision of the Wechsler-Bellevue test (1939), standardized for use with adults over the age of 16.
Wechsler Preschool and Primary Scale of Intelligence	The Wechsler Preschool and Primary Scale of intelligence is an IQ test for young children that measures a range of performance, verbal, and preverbal abilities for children from 3 to

Paradoxical	Paradoxical intention refers to instructing clients to do the opposite of the desired behavior. Telling an impotent man not to have sex or an insomniac not to sleep reduces anxiety to perform.
Deductive reasoning	Deductive reasoning refers to a form of reasoning about arguments in which conclusions are determined from the premises. The conclusions are true if the premises are true.
Ethnicity	Ethnicity refers to a characteristic based on cultural heritage, nationality characteristics, race, religion, and language.
Variable	A variable refers to a measurable factor, characteristic, or attribute of an individual or a system.
Coding	In senation, coding is the process by which information about the quality and quantity of a stimulus is preserved in the pattern of action potentials sent through sensory neurons to the central nervous system.
Kaufman assessment battery for children	The Kaufman assessment battery for children is a nontraditional individual intelligence test designed to provide fair assessments of minority children and children with disabilities.
Information processing	Information processing is an approach to the goal of understanding human thinking. The essence of the approach is to see cognition as being essentially computational in nature, with mind being the software and the brain being the hardware.
Cognitive psychology	Cognitive psychology is the psychological science which studies the mental processes that are hypothesised to underlie behavior. This covers a broad range of research domains, examining questions about the workings of memory, attention, perception, knowledge representation, reasoning, creativity and problem solving.
Reading comprehension	Reading comprehension can be defined as the level of understanding of a passage or text. For normal reading rates (around 200-220 words per minute) an acceptable level of comprehension is above 75%.
Innate	Innate behavior is not learned or influenced by the environment, rather, it is present or predisposed at birth.
Achievement test	A test designed to determine a person's level of knowledge in a given subject area is referred to as an achievement test.
Crystallized intelligence	One's lifetime of intellectual achievement, as and shown largely through vocabulary and knowledge of world affairs is called crystallized intelligence.
Acculturation	Acculturation is the obtainment of culture by an individual or a group of people.
Piaget	Piaget argued that young children's answers were qualitatively different than older children rather than quantitative. There are two major aspects to his theory: the process of coming to know and the stages we move through as we gradually acquire this ability.
Psychometric	Psychometric study is concerned with the theory and technique of psychological measurement, which includes the measurement of knowledge, abilities, attitudes, and personality traits. The field is primarily concerned with the study of differences between individuals
Expressive vocabulary	The total number of words that one can use in the production of language is called their expressive vocabulary.
Stimulus	A change in an environmental condition that elicits a response is a stimulus.
Empirical	Empirical means the use of working hypotheses which are capable of being disproved using observation or experiment.

Go to **Cram101.com** for the Practice Tests for this Chapter.
And, **NEVER** highlight a book again!

Demographic variable	A varying characteristic that is a vital or social statistic of an individual, sample group, or population, for example, age, sex, socioeconomic status, racial origin, education is called a demographic variable.
Homogeneous	In biology homogeneous has a meaning similar to its meaning in mathematics. Generally it means "the same" or "of the same quality or general property".
Statistic	A statistic is an observable random variable of a sample.
Internal validity	Internal validity is a term pertaining to scientific research that signifies the extent to which the conditions within a research design were conducive to drawing the conclusions the researcher was interested in drawing.
Variance	The degree to which scores differ among individuals in a distribution of scores is the variance.

Go to **Cram101.com** for the Practice Tests for this Chapter.

Go to **Cram101.com** for the Practice Tests for this Chapter.
And, **NEVER** highlight a book again!

Prototype	A concept of a category of objects or events that serves as a good example of the category is called a prototype.
Yerkes	Yerkes worked in the field of comparative psychology. He is best known for studying the intelligence and social behavior of gorillas and chimpanzees. Joining with John D. Dodson, he developed the Yerkes-Dodson law relating arousal to performance.
Population	Population refers to all members of a well-defined group of organisms, events, or things.
Wechsler Scales	The Wechsler Scales are two well-known intelligence scales, namely the Wechsler Adult Intelligence Scale and the Wechsler Intelligence Scale for Children.
Subculture	As understood in sociology, anthropology and cultural studies, a subculture is a set of people with a distinct set of behavior and beliefs that differentiate them from a larger culture of which they are a part.
Intelligence test	An intelligence test is a standardized means of assessing a person's current mental ability, for example, the Stanford-Binet test and the Wechsler Adult Intelligence Scale.
Sensorimotor	The first of Piaget's stages is the Sensorimotor stage. This stage typically ranges from birth to 2 years. In this stage, children experience the world through their senses. During this stage, object permanence and stranger anxiety develop.
Stimulus	A change in an environmental condition that elicits a response is a stimulus.
Trait	An enduring personality characteristic that tends to lead to certain behaviors is called a trait. The term trait also means a genetically inherited feature of an organism.
Wechsler Preschool and Primary Scale of Intelligence	The Wechsler Preschool and Primary Scale of intelligence is an IQ test for young children that measures a range of performance, verbal, and preverbal abilities for children from 3 to
Arnold Gesell	Arnold Gesell was a pioneer in the field of child development and developmental measurement. He constructed the Gesell dome, a one-way mirror shaped as a dome, under which children could be observed without being disturbed.
Direct observation	Direct observation refers to assessing behavior through direct surveillance.
Standardized test	An oral or written assessment for which an individual receives a score indicating how the individual reponded relative to a previously tested large sample of others is referred to as a standardized test.
Early childhood	Early childhood refers to the developmental period extending from the end of infancy to about 5 or 6 years of age; sometimes called the preschool years.
Bayley Scales	The Bayley Scales of Infant Development are widely used in assessing infant development for infants 1-42 months of age. The current version has three parts: a Mental Scale, a Motor Scale, and the Infant Behavior Profile. Among the uses are the diagnosis of developmental delays and the planning of intervention strategies.
Problem solving	An attempt to find an appropriate way of attaining a goal when the goal is not readily available is called problem solving.
Learning	Learning is a relatively permanent change in behavior that results from experience. Thus, to attribute a behavioral change to learning, the change must be relatively permanent and must result from experience.
Infancy	The developmental period that extends from birth to 18 or 24 months is called infancy.
Mental processes	The thoughts, feelings, and motives that each of us experiences privately but that cannot be

observed directly are called mental processes.

Personality	Personality refers to the pattern of enduring characteristics that differentiates a person, the patterns of behaviors that make each individual unique.
Attention	Attention is the cognitive process of selectively concentrating on one thing while ignoring other things. Psychologists have labeled three types of attention: sustained attention, selective attention, and divided attention.
Norms	In testing, standards of test performance that permit the comparison of one person's score on the test to the scores of others who have taken the same test are referred to as norms.
Percentile rank	The percentile rank of a score is the percentage of scores in its frequency distribution which are lower.
Discrimination	In Learning theory, discrimination refers the ability to distinguish between a conditioned stimulus and other stimuli. It can be brought about by extensive training or differential reinforcement. In social terms, it is the denial of privileges to a person or a group on the basis of prejudice.
Psychometric	Psychometric study is concerned with the theory and technique of psychological measurement, which includes the measurement of knowledge, abilities, attitudes, and personality traits. The field is primarily concerned with the study of differences between individuals
Quantitative	A quantitative property is one that exists in a range of magnitudes, and can therefore be measured. Measurements of any particular quantitative property are expressed as as a specific quantity, referred to as a unit, multiplied by a number.
Etiology	Etiology is the study of causation. The term is used in philosophy, physics and biology in reference to the causes of various phenomena. It is generally the study of why things occur, or even the reasons behind the way that things act.
Validity	The extent to which a test measures what it is intended to measure is called validity.
Theories	Theories are logically self-consistent models or frameworks describing the behavior of a certain natural or social phenomenon. They are broad explanations and predictions concerning phenomena of interest.
Piaget	Piaget argued that young children's answers were qualitatively different than older children rather than quantitative. There are two major aspects to his theory: the process of coming to know and the stages we move through as we gradually acquire this ability.
Psychological testing	Psychological testing is a field characterized by the use of small samples of behavior in order to infer larger generalizations about a given individual. The technical term for psychological testing is psychometrics.
Developmental psychology	The branch of psychology that studies the patterns of growth and change occurring throughout life is referred to as developmental psychology.
Concrete operational	According to Piaget, the period from 7 to 12 years of age, which is characterized by logical thought and a loss of egocentrism, is referred to as concrete operational stage. Conservation skills are formed - understanding that quantity, length or number of items is unrelated to the appearance of the object or items.
Formal operational	According to Piaget, the period from age 12 to adulthood, which is characterized by abstract thought is referred to as the formal operational stage.
Ordinal scale	An ordinal scale defines a total preorder of objects; using ranks instead of actual numbers.
Stages	Stages represent relatively discrete periods of time in which functioning is qualitatively different from functioning at other periods.

Go to **Cram101.com** for the Practice Tests for this Chapter.

Object permanence	Object permanence is the term used to describe the awareness that objects continue to exist even when they are no longer visible. According to Piaget, object permance for the infant develops once the sensorimotor stage is complete.
Object relation	Object relation theory is the idea that the ego-self exists only in relation to other objects, which may be external or internal.
Schemata	Cognitive categories or frames of reference are called schemata.
Schema	Schema refers to a way of mentally representing the world, such as a belief or an expectation, that can influence perception of persons, objects, and situations.
Variable	A variable refers to a measurable factor, characteristic, or attribute of an individual or a system.
Conservation	Conservation refers to the recognition that basic properties of substances such as weight and mass remain the same even when transformations merely alter their appearance.
Clinical assessment	A clinical assessment is a systematic evaluation and measurement of psychological, biological, and social factors in a person presenting with a possible psychological disorder.
Correlation	A statistical technique for determining the degree of association between two or more variables is referred to as correlation.
Piagetian approach	A Piagetian approach is the study of cognitive development where there are a distinct sequence of qualitative critical stages that are met biologically, experientially, and cognitively.
Construct validity	The extent to which there is evidence that a test measures a particular hypothetical construct is referred to as construct validity.
Construct	A generalized concept, such as anxiety or gravity, is a construct.
Cognitive development	The process by which a child's understanding of the world changes as a function of age and experience is called cognitive development.
Empirical	Empirical means the use of working hypotheses which are capable of being disproved using observation or experiment.
Affect	A subjective feeling or emotional tone often accompanied by bodily expressions noticeable to others is called affect.
Information processing	Information processing is an approach to the goal of understanding human thinking. The essence of the approach is to see cognition as being essentially computational in nature, with mind being the software and the brain being the hardware.
Knowledge base	The general background information a person possesses, which influences most cognitive task performance is called the knowledge base.
Mental retardation	Mental retardation refers to having significantly below-average intellectual functioning and limitations in at least two areas of adaptive functioning. Many categorize retardation as mild, moderate, severe, or profound.
Social skills	Social skills are skills used to interact and communicate with others to assist status in the social structure and other motivations.
Individuals with Disabilities Education Act	The Individuals with Disabilities Education Act is a United States law meant to ensure "a free appropriate public education" for students with disabilities, designed to their individualized needs in the Least Restricted Environment.
Early	Early intervention is a process used to recognize warning signs for mental health problems

Intervention	and to take early action against factors that put individuals at risk.
Standard deviation	In probability and statistics, the standard deviation is the most commonly used measure of statistical dispersion. Simply put, it measures how spread out the values in a data set are.
Threshold	In general, a threshold is a fixed location or value where an abrupt change is observed. In the sensory modalities, it is the minimum amount of stimulus energy necessary to elicit a sensory response.
Acute	Acute means sudden, sharp, and abrupt. Usually short in duration.
Diagnostic and Statistical Manual of Mental Disorders	The Diagnostic and Statistical Manual of Mental Disorders, published by the American Psychiatric Association, is the handbook used most often in diagnosing mental disorders in the United States and internationally.
Mental disorder	Mental disorder refers to a disturbance in a person's emotions, drives, thought processes, or behavior that involves serious and relatively prolonged distress and/or impairment in ability to function, is not simply a normal response to some event or set of events in the person's environment.
Adaptive behavior	An adaptive behavior increases the probability of the individual or organism to survive or exist within its environment.
Vineland adaptive behavior scale	Vineland adaptive behavior scale is an instrument for assessing how many age appropriate, socially adaptive behaviors a child engages in.
Survey	A method of scientific investigation in which a large sample of people answer questions about their attitudes or behavior is referred to as a survey.
Maladaptive	In psychology, a behavior or trait is adaptive when it helps an individual adjust and function well within their social environment. A maladaptive behavior or trait is counterproductive to the individual.
Ethnic group	An ethnic group is a culture or subculture whose members are readily distinguishable by outsiders based on traits originating from a common racial, national, linguistic, or religious source. Members of an ethnic group are often presumed to be culturally or biologically similar, although this is not in fact necessarily the case.
Raw score	A raw score is an original datum that has not been transformed – for example, the original result obtained by a student on a test (i.e., the number of correctly answered items) as opposed to that score after transformation to a standard score or percentile rank or the like.
Median	The median is a number that separates the higher half of a sample, a population, or a probability distribution from the lower half. It is the middle value in a distribution, above and below which lie an equal number of values.
Test-retest reliability	The consistency of a measure when it is repeated over time is called test-retest reliability. It involves administering the test to the same group of people at least twice. The first set of scores is correlated with the second set of scores. Correlations range between 0 (low reliability) and 1 (high reliability).
Reliability	Reliability means the extent to which a test produces a consistent , reproducible score .
Factor analysis	Factor analysis is a statistical technique that originated in psychometrics. The objective is to explain the most of the variability among a number of observable random variables in terms of a smaller number of unobservable random variables called factors.

Go to **Cram101.com** for the Practice Tests for this Chapter.

Accommodation	Piaget's developmental process of accommodation is the modification of currently held schemes or new schemes so that new information inconsistent with the existing schemes can be integrated and understood.
Adaptation	Adaptation is a lowering of sensitivity to a stimulus following prolonged exposure to that stimulus. Behavioral adaptations are special ways a particular organism behaves to survive in its natural habitat.
Sullivan	Sullivan developed the Self System, a configuration of the personality traits developed in childhood and reinforced by positive affirmation and the security operations developed in childhood to avoid anxiety and threats to self-esteem.
Evolution	Commonly used to refer to gradual change, evolution is the change in the frequency of alleles within a population from one generation to the next. This change may be caused by different mechanisms, including natural selection, genetic drift, or changes in population (gene flow).
Scholastic Assessment Test	The Scholastic Assessment Test is a standardized test frequently used by colleges and universities to aid in the selection of incoming students.
Stanford-Binet	Terman released the "Stanford Revision of the Binet-Simon Scale" or the Stanford-Binet for short. Using validation experiments, he removed several of the Binet-Simon test items and added new ones. In 1985 it was revised to analyze an individual's responses in four content areas: verbal reasoning, quantitative reasoning, abstract reasoning, and short-term memory.
Aptitude test	A test designed to predict a person's ability in a particular area or line of work is called an aptitude test.
Normative	The term normative is used to describe the effects of those structures of culture which regulate the function of social activity.
Tactile	Pertaining to the sense of touch is referred to as tactile.
Cerebral palsy	Cerebral palsy is a group of permanent disorders associated with developmental brain injuries that occur during fetal development, birth, or shortly after birth. It is characterized by a disruption of motor skills, with symptoms such as spasticity, paralysis, or seizures.
Individual intelligence test	A test of intelligence designed to be given to a single individual by a trained specialist is an individual intelligence test. Background information supplements the test.
Verbal intelligence	Verbal intelligence is measured by answering questions involving vocabulary , general information , arithmetic , and other languageor symbol-oriented tasks.
Achievement test	A test designed to determine a person's level of knowledge in a given subject area is referred to as an achievement test.
Assimilation	According to Piaget, assimilation is the process of the organism interacting with the environment given the organism's cognitive structure. Assimilation is reuse of schemas to fit new information.
Basic research	Basic research has as its primary objective the advancement of knowledge and the theoretical understanding of the relations among variables . It is exploratory and often driven by the researcher's curiosity, interest or hunch.
Motivation	In psychology, motivation is the driving force (desire) behind all actions of an organism.
Reasoning	Reasoning is the act of using reason to derive a conclusion from certain premises. There are two main methods to reach a conclusion,deductive reasoning and inductive reasoning.
Divided attention	Concentrating on more than one activity at a time is divided attention. The ability to shift attention as required is more difficult for younger versus older children.

G factor	Spearman's term for a general intellectual ability that underlies all mental operations to some degree is called the g factor.
Heterogeneous	A heterogeneous compound, mixture, or other such object is one that consists of many different items, which are often not easily sorted or separated, though they are clearly distinct.
Homogeneous	In biology homogeneous has a meaning similar to its meaning in mathematics. Generally it means "the same" or "of the same quality or general property".
Concurrent validity	Concurrent validity is demonstrated where a test correlates well with a measure that has previously been validated.
Predictive validity	Predictive validity refers to the relation between test scores and the student 's future performance .
Inductive reasoning	A form of reasoning in which we reason from individual cases or particular facts to a general conclusion is referred to as inductive reasoning. The conclusion can be said to follow with a probability rather than certainty.
Projective test	A projective test is a personality test designed to let a person respond to ambiguous stimuli, presumably revealing hidden emotions and internal conflicts. This is different from an "objective test" in which responses are analyzed according to a universal standard rather than an individual psychiatrist's judgement.
Positive correlation	A relationship between two variables in which both vary in the same direction is called a positive correlation.
Socioeconomic Status	A family's socioeconomic status is based on family income, parental education level, parental occupation, and social status in the community. Those with high status often have more success in preparing their children for school because they have access to a wide range of resources.
Socioeconomic	Socioeconomic pertains to the study of the social and economic impacts of any product or service offering, market intervention or other activity on an economy as a whole and on the companies, organization and individuals who are its main economic actors.
Culture-fair	An intelligence test that does not discriminate against members of any minority group is called culture-fair.
Counseling psychologist	A doctoral level mental health professional whose training is similar to that of a clinical psychologist, though usually with less emphasis on research and serious psychopathology is referred to as a counseling psychologist.
Individual differences	Individual differences psychology studies the ways in which individual people differ in their behavior. This is distinguished from other aspects of psychology in that although psychology is ostensibly a study of individuals, modern psychologists invariably study groups.
Anxiety	Anxiety is a complex combination of the feeling of fear, apprehension and worry often accompanied by physical sensations such as palpitations, chest pain and/or shortness of breath.
Acculturation	Acculturation is the obtainment of culture by an individual or a group of people.
Cognitive skills	Cognitive skills such as reasoning, attention, and memory can be advanced and sustained through practice and training.
Psychological test	Psychological test refers to a standardized measure of a sample of a person's behavior.
Social class	Social class describes the relationships between people in hierarchical societies or

cultures. Those with more power usually subordinate those with less power.

Conformity   Conformity is the degree to which members of a group will change their behavior, views and attitudes to fit the views of the group. The group can influence members via unconscious processes or via overt social pressure on individuals.

Creativity   Creativity is the ability to think about something in novel and unusual ways and come up with unique solutions to problems. It involves divergent thinking, having many solutions or views to a problem.

101

Wechsler Scales	The Wechsler Scales are two well-known intelligence scales, namely the Wechsler Adult Intelligence Scale and the Wechsler Intelligence Scale for Children.
Stanford-Binet	Terman released the "Stanford Revision of the Binet-Simon Scale" or the Stanford-Binet for short. Using validation experiments, he removed several of the Binet-Simon test items and added new ones. In 1985 it was revised to analyze an individual's responses in four content areas: verbal reasoning, quantitative reasoning, abstract reasoning, and short-term memory.
Affect	A subjective feeling or emotional tone often accompanied by bodily expressions noticeable to others is called affect.
Variance	The degree to which scores differ among individuals in a distribution of scores is the variance.
Norms	In testing, standards of test performance that permit the comparison of one person's score on the test to the scores of others who have taken the same test are referred to as norms.
Representative sample	Representative sample refers to a sample of participants selected from the larger population in such a way that important subgroups within the population are included in the sample in the same proportions as they are found in the larger population.
Normative	The term normative is used to describe the effects of those structures of culture which regulate the function of social activity.
Anxiety	Anxiety is a complex combination of the feeling of fear, apprehension and worry often accompanied by physical sensations such as palpitations, chest pain and/or shortness of breath.
Validity	The extent to which a test measures what it is intended to measure is called validity.
Piagetian approach	A Piagetian approach is the study of cognitive development where there are a distinct sequence of qualitative critical stages that are met biologically, experientially, and cognitively.
Direct observation	Direct observation refers to assessing behavior through direct surveillance.
Response-contingent	Reinforcement, punishment, or other consequences that are applied only when a certain response is made are response-contingent consequences.
Standard error of measurement	The estimate of the 'error' associated with the test-taker's obtained score when compared with their hypothetical 'true' score is standard error of measurement. The standard error of measurement, which varies from test to test, should be given in the test manual.
Psychometric	Psychometric study is concerned with the theory and technique of psychological measurement, which includes the measurement of knowledge, abilities, attitudes, and personality traits. The field is primarily concerned with the study of differences between individuals
Reliability	Reliability means the extent to which a test produces a consistent , reproducible score .
Correlation	A statistical technique for determining the degree of association between two or more variables is referred to as correlation.
Test standardization	A technique used to validate questions in personality tests by studying the responses of people with known diagnoses, is referred to as test standardization.
Standardized test	An oral or written assessment for which an individual receives a score indicating how the individual reponded relative to a previously tested large sample of others is referred to as a standardized test.
Quantitative	A quantitative property is one that exists in a range of magnitudes, and can therefore be measured. Measurements of any particular quantitative property are expressed as as a specific

quantity, referred to as a unit, multiplied by a number.

Predictive validity	Predictive validity refers to the relation between test scores and the student 's future performance .
Achievement test	A test designed to determine a person's level of knowledge in a given subject area is referred to as an achievement test.
Cognitive skills	Cognitive skills such as reasoning, attention, and memory can be advanced and sustained through practice and training.
Attention	Attention is the cognitive process of selectively concentrating on one thing while ignoring other things. Psychologists have labeled three types of attention: sustained attention, selective attention, and divided attention.
Reasoning	Reasoning is the act of using reason to derive a conclusion from certain premises. There are two main methods to reach a conclusion,deductive reasoning and inductive reasoning.
Discrimination	In Learning theory, discrimination refers the ability to distinguish between a conditioned stimulus and other stimuli. It can be brought about by extensive training or differential reinforcement. In social terms, it is the denial of privileges to a person or a group on the basis of prejudice.
Nonsense syllable	A nonsense syllable is a consonant-vowel-consonant combination that does not spell a word. It is an expermental methodology invented by Ebbinghaus to control for the meaningfulness of the material in studies of memory.
Trait	An enduring personality characteristic that tends to lead to certain behaviors is called a trait. The term trait also means a genetically inherited feature of an organism.
Cognitive development	The process by which a child's understanding of the world changes as a function of age and experience is called cognitive development.
Intelligence test	An intelligence test is a standardized means of assessing a person's current mental ability, for example, the Stanford-Binet test and the Wechsler Adult Intelligence Scale.
Practical intelligence	Practical intelligence focuses on the ability to use, apply, implement, and put into practice.
Reflection	Reflection is the process of rephrasing or repeating thoughts and feelings expressed, making the person more aware of what they are saying or thinking.
Factor analysis	Factor analysis is a statistical technique that originated in psychometrics. The objective is to explain the most of the variability among a number of observable random variables in terms of a smaller number of unobservable random variables called factors.
Aptitude test	A test designed to predict a person's ability in a particular area or line of work is called an aptitude test.
Wechsler Adult Intelligence Scale	Wechsler adult intelligence scale is an individual intelligence test for adults that yields separate verbal and performance IQ scores as well as an overall IQ score.
Wechsler adult Intelligence	Wechsler adult Intelligence Scale is a revision of the Wechsler-Bellevue test (1939), standardized for use with adults over the age of 16.
Heterogeneous	A heterogeneous compound, mixture, or other such object is one that consists of many different items, which are often not easily sorted or separated, though they are clearly distinct.
Empirical	Empirical means the use of working hypotheses which are capable of being disproved using observation or experiment.

Go to **Cram101.com** for the Practice Tests for this Chapter.

Psychological test	Psychological test refers to a standardized measure of a sample of a person's behavior.
Educational psychology	Educational psychology is the study of how children and adults learn, the effectiveness of various educational strategies and tactics, and how schools function as organizations.
Sternberg	Sternberg proposed the triarchic theory of intelligence: componential, experiential, and practical. His notion of general intelligence or the g-factor, is a composite of intelligence scores across multiple modalities.
Survey	A method of scientific investigation in which a large sample of people answer questions about their attitudes or behavior is referred to as a survey.
Intelligence test	An intelligence test is a standardized means of assessing a person's current mental ability, for example, the Stanford-Binet test and the Wechsler Adult Intelligence Scale.
Affect	A subjective feeling or emotional tone often accompanied by bodily expressions noticeable to others is called affect.
Norms	In testing, standards of test performance that permit the comparison of one person's score on the test to the scores of others who have taken the same test are referred to as norms.
Gender difference	A gender difference is a disparity between genders involving quality or quantity. Though some gender differences are controversial, they are not to be confused with sexist stereotypes.
Stereotype	A stereotype is considered to be a group concept, held by one social group about another. They are often used in a negative or prejudicial sense and are frequently used to justify certain discriminatory behaviors. This allows powerful social groups to legitimize and protect their dominant position
Herrnstein	Herrnstein was a prominent researcher in comparative psychology who did pioneering work on pigeon intelligence employing the Experimental Analysis of Behavior and formulated the "Matching Law" in the 1960s, a breakthrough in understanding how reinforcement and behavior are linked.
American Psychological Association	The American Psychological Association is a professional organization representing psychology in the US. The mission statement is to "advance psychology as a science and profession and as a means of promoting health, education , and human welfare".
Intelligence quotient	An intelligence quotient is a score derived from a set of standardized tests that were developed with the purpose of measuring a person's cognitive abilities ("intelligence") in relation to their age group.
Chronological age	Chronological age refers to the number of years that have elapsed since a person's birth.
Mental age	The mental age refers to the accumulated months of credit that a person earns on the Stanford-Binet Intelligence Scale.
Self-understanding	Self-understanding is a child's cognitive representation of the self, the substance and content of the child's self-conceptions.
Attention	Attention is the cognitive process of selectively concentrating on one thing while ignoring other things. Psychologists have labeled three types of attention: sustained attention, selective attention, and divided attention.
Infancy	The developmental period that extends from birth to 18 or 24 months is called infancy.
Subculture	As understood in sociology, anthropology and cultural studies, a subculture is a set of people with a distinct set of behavior and beliefs that differentiate them from a larger culture of which they are a part.

Go to **Cram101.com** for the Practice Tests for this Chapter.

Reflection	Reflection is the process of rephrasing or repeating thoughts and feelings expressed, making the person more aware of what they are saying or thinking.
Variable	A variable refers to a measurable factor, characteristic, or attribute of an individual or a system.
Validity	The extent to which a test measures what it is intended to measure is called validity.
Construct	A generalized concept, such as anxiety or gravity, is a construct.
Factor analysis	Factor analysis is a statistical technique that originated in psychometrics. The objective is to explain the most of the variability among a number of observable random variables in terms of a smaller number of unobservable random variables called factors.
Heritability	Heritability It is that proportion of the observed variation in a particular phenotype within a particular population, that can be attributed to the contribution of genotype. In other words: it measures the extent to which differences between individuals in a population are due their being different genetically.
Trait	An enduring personality characteristic that tends to lead to certain behaviors is called a trait. The term trait also means a genetically inherited feature of an organism.
Correlation	A statistical technique for determining the degree of association between two or more variables is referred to as correlation.
Monozygotic	Identical twins occur when a single egg is fertilized to form one zygote, calld monozygotic, but the zygote then divides into two separate embryos. The two embryos develop into foetuses sharing the same womb. Monozygotic twins are genetically identical unless there has been a mutation in development, and they are almost always the same gender.
Dizygotic	Fraternal twins (commonly known as "non-identical twins") usually occur when two fertilized eggs are implanted in the uterine wall at the same time. The two eggs form two zygotes, and these twins are therefore also known as dizygotic.
Bronfenbrenner	Bronfenbrenner was a co-founder of the U.S. national Head Start program and founder of the Ecological Theory of Development.
Severe mental retardation	A limitation in mental development as measured on the Wechsler Adult Intelligence Scale with scores between 20 -34 is called severe mental retardation.
Mental retardation	Mental retardation refers to having significantly below-average intellectual functioning and limitations in at least two areas of adaptive functioning. Many categorize retardation as mild, moderate, severe, or profound.
Population	Population refers to all members of a well-defined group of organisms, events, or things.
Prenatal	Prenatal period refers to the time from conception to birth.
Trauma	Trauma refers to a severe physical injury or wound to the body caused by an external force, or a psychological shock having a lasting effect on mental life.
Hebb	Hebb demonstrated that the rearing of rats in an enriched environment could alter neural development and that sensory - neural connections were shaped by experience. He is famous for developing the concept of neural nets. He also believed that learning early in life is of the incremental variety, whereas later it is cognitive, insightful, and more all-or-none.
Phenylketonuria	Phenylketonuria is a genetic disorder in which an individual cannot properly metabolize amino acids. The disorder is now easily detected but, if left untreated, results in mental retardation and hyperactivity.
Deprivation	Deprivation, is the loss or withholding of normal stimulation, nutrition, comfort, love, and so forth; a condition of lacking. The level of stimulation is less than what is required.

Brain	The brain controls and coordinates most movement, behavior and homeostatic body functions such as heartbeat, blood pressure, fluid balance and body temperature. Functions of the brain are responsible for cognition, emotion, memory, motor learning and other sorts of learning. The brain is primarily made up of two types of cells: glia and neurons.
Gene	A gene is an ultramicroscopic area of the chromosome. It is the smallest physical unit of the DNA molecule that carries a piece of hereditary information.
Empirical	Empirical means the use of working hypotheses which are capable of being disproved using observation or experiment.
Cognitive skills	Cognitive skills such as reasoning, attention, and memory can be advanced and sustained through practice and training.
Aptitude test	A test designed to predict a person's ability in a particular area or line of work is called an aptitude test.
Learning	Learning is a relatively permanent change in behavior that results from experience. Thus, to attribute a behavioral change to learning, the change must be relatively permanent and must result from experience.
Baltes	Baltes describes the life-span perspective as one that sees hurman development as lifelong, multidimensional, multidirectional, plastic, contextual, and multidisciplinary, and as involving growth, maintenance, and regulation.
Habit	A habit is a response that has become completely separated from its eliciting stimulus. Early learning theorists used the term to describe S-R associations, however not all S-R associations become a habit, rather many are extinguished after reinforcement is withdrawn.
Generalizability	The ability to extend a set of findings observed in one piece of research to other situations and groups is called generalizability.
Schema	Schema refers to a way of mentally representing the world, such as a belief or an expectation, that can influence perception of persons, objects, and situations.
Motivation	In psychology, motivation is the driving force (desire) behind all actions of an organism.
Personality	Personality refers to the pattern of enduring characteristics that differentiates a person, the patterns of behaviors that make each individual unique.
Self-concept	Self-concept refers to domain-specific evaluations of the self where a domain may be academics, athletics, etc.
Attitude	An enduring mental representation of a person, place, or thing that evokes an emotional response and related behavior is called attitude.
Modeling	A type of behavior learned through observation of others demonstrating the same behavior is modeling.
Affective	Affective is the way people react emotionally, their ability to feel another living thing's pain or joy.
Achievement motivation	The psychological need in humans for success is called achievement motivation.
Simulation	A simulation is an imitation of some real device or state of affairs. Simulation attempts to represent certain features of the behavior of a physical or abstract system by the behavior of another system.
Personality test	A personality test aims to describe aspects of a person's character that remain stable across situations.

Go to **Cram101.com** for the Practice Tests for this Chapter.

Personality trait	According to the Diagnostic and Statistical Manual of the American Psychiatric Association, a personality trait is a "prominent aspect of personality that is exhibited in a wide range of important social and personal contexts. ...".
Cognitive development	The process by which a child's understanding of the world changes as a function of age and experience is called cognitive development.
Reading comprehension	Reading comprehension can be defined as the level of understanding of a passage or text. For normal reading rates (around 200-220 words per minute) an acceptable level of comprehension is above 75%.
Postulates	Postulates are general statements about behavior that cannot be directly verified. They are used to generate theorems which can be tested.
Positive manifold	In psychometric approaches to intelligence, the high correlations among scores on sets of cognitive tests that have little in common with one another in terms of content or types of strategies used is referred to as a positive manifold.
Thurstone	Thurstone was a pioneer in the field of psychometrics. His work in factor analysis led him to formulate a model of intelligence center around "Primary Mental Abilities", which were independent group factors of intelligence that different individuals possessed in varying degrees.
Invariance	Invariance is the property of perception whereby simple geometrical objects are recognized independent of rotation, translation, and scale, as well as several other variations such as elastic deformations, different lighting, and different component features.
Variance	The degree to which scores differ among individuals in a distribution of scores is the variance.
Reliability	Reliability means the extent to which a test produces a consistent , reproducible score .
Reasoning	Reasoning is the act of using reason to derive a conclusion from certain premises. There are two main methods to reach a conclusion,deductive reasoning and inductive reasoning.
Positive correlation	A relationship between two variables in which both vary in the same direction is called a positive correlation.
G factor	Spearman's term for a general intellectual ability that underlies all mental operations to some degree is called the g factor.
Theories	Theories are logically self-consistent models or frameworks describing the behavior of a certain natural or social phenomenon. They are broad explanations and predictions concerning phenomena of interest.
Psychological testing	Psychological testing is a field characterized by the use of small samples of behavior in order to infer larger generalizations about a given individual. The technical term for psychological testing is psychometrics.
Multiple-factor theory	Multiple-factor theory is Thurstone's theory that intelligence consists of seven primary mental abilities: verbal comprehension, number ability, word fluency, spatial visualization, associative memory, reasoning, and perceptual speed.
Primary mental abilities	According to Thurstone, the basic abilities that make up intelligence are called primary mental abilities.
Guilford	Guilford observed that most individuals display a preference for either convergent or divergent thinking. Scientists and engineers typically prefer the former and artists and performers, the latter.
Divergent	A thought process that attempts to generate multiple solutions to problems is called

Go to **Cram101.com** for the Practice Tests for this Chapter.

thinking	divergent thinking.
Cognition	The intellectual processes through which information is obtained, transformed, stored, retrieved, and otherwise used is cognition.
Creativity	Creativity is the ability to think about something in novel and unusual ways and come up with unique solutions to problems. It involves divergent thinking, having many solutions or views to a problem.
Elaboration	The extensiveness of processing at any given level of memory is called elaboration. The use of elaboration changes developmentally. Adolescents are more likely to use elaboration spontaneously than children.
Heterogeneous	A heterogeneous compound, mixture, or other such object is one that consists of many different items, which are often not easily sorted or separated, though they are clearly distinct.
Socioeconomic	Socioeconomic pertains to the study of the social and economic impacts of any product or service offering, market intervention or other activity on an economy as a whole and on the companies, organization and individuals who are its main economic actors.
Individual differences	Individual differences psychology studies the ways in which individual people differ in their behavior. This is distinguished from other aspects of psychology in that although psychology is ostensibly a study of individuals, modern psychologists invariably study groups.
Transfer of training	The concept of transfer of training states that knowledge or abilities acquired in one area aids the acquisition of knowledge or abilities in other areas. When prior learning is helpful, it is called positive transfer. When prior learning inhibits new learning, it is called negative transfer.
Harlow	Harlow and his famous wire and cloth surrogate mother monkey studies demonstrated that the need for affection created a stronger bond between mother and infant than did physical needs. He also found that the more discrimination problems the monkeys solved, the better they became at solving them.
Cognitive psychology	Cognitive psychology is the psychological science which studies the mental processes that are hypothesised to underlie behavior. This covers a broad range of research domains, examining questions about the workings of memory, attention, perception, knowledge representation, reasoning, creativity and problem solving.
Retrieval	Retrieval is the location of stored information and its subsequent return to consciousness. It is the third stage of information processing.
Associative memory	Associative memory is a non Von Neumann computing architecture. It is characterized by the fact that each address in an associative memory has a small amount of computing power.
Practical intelligence	Practical intelligence focuses on the ability to use, apply, implement, and put into practice.
Csikszentmihalyi	Csikszentmihalyi is noted for his work in the study of happiness, creativity, subjective well-being, and fun, but is best known for his having been the architect of the notion of flow: "... people are most happy when they are in a state of flow--a Zen-like state of total oneness...".
Terman	Terman revised the Stanford-Binet Intelligence Scale in 1916, commonly used to measure intelligence (or I.Q.) in the United States. William Stern's suggestion that mental age/chronological age times 100 (to get rid of the decimal) be made the "intelligence quotient" or I.Q. This apparent mathematization of the measurement gave it an air of scientific accuracy and detachment which contributed greatly to its acceptance among educators and the broad public.

Go to **Cram101.com** for the Practice Tests for this Chapter.

95

Go to **Cram101.com** for the Practice Tests for this Chapter.

Attention	Attention is the cognitive process of selectively concentrating on one thing while ignoring other things. Psychologists have labeled three types of attention: sustained attention, selective attention, and divided attention.
Construct	A generalized concept, such as anxiety or gravity, is a construct.
Intelligence test	An intelligence test is a standardized means of assessing a person's current mental ability, for example, the Stanford-Binet test and the Wechsler Adult Intelligence Scale.
Reliability	Reliability means the extent to which a test produces a consistent , reproducible score .
Correlation	A statistical technique for determining the degree of association between two or more variables is referred to as correlation.
Population	Population refers to all members of a well-defined group of organisms, events, or things.
Longitudinal study	Longitudinal study is a type of developmental study in which the same group of participants is followed and measured for an extended period of time, often years.
Stanford-Binet	Terman released the "Stanford Revision of the Binet-Simon Scale" or the Stanford-Binet for short. Using validation experiments, he removed several of the Binet-Simon test items and added new ones. In 1985 it was revised to analyze an individual's responses in four content areas: verbal reasoning, quantitative reasoning, abstract reasoning, and short-term memory.
Acquisition	Acquisition is the process of adapting to the environment, learning or becoming conditioned. In classical conditoning terms, it is the initial learning of the stimulus response link, which involves a neutral stimulus being associated with a unconditioned stimulus and becoming a conditioned stimulus.
Socioeconomic	Socioeconomic pertains to the study of the social and economic impacts of any product or service offering, market intervention or other activity on an economy as a whole and on the companies, organization and individuals who are its main economic actors.
Learning	Learning is a relatively permanent change in behavior that results from experience. Thus, to attribute a behavioral change to learning, the change must be relatively permanent and must result from experience.
Piagetian approach	A Piagetian approach is the study of cognitive development where there are a distinct sequence of qualitative critical stages that are met biologically, experientially, and cognitively.
Project head start	Project Head Start is a program of the US government's Department of Health and Human Services which focuses on assisting low-income children, through five years of age; so that they are prepared for school.
Quantitative	A quantitative property is one that exists in a range of magnitudes, and can therefore be measured. Measurements of any particular quantitative property are expressed as as a specific quantity, referred to as a unit, multiplied by a number.
Self-concept	Self-concept refers to domain-specific evaluations of the self where a domain may be academics, athletics, etc.
Personality	Personality refers to the pattern of enduring characteristics that differentiates a person, the patterns of behaviors that make each individual unique.
Motivation	In psychology, motivation is the driving force (desire) behind all actions of an organism.
Attitude	An enduring mental representation of a person, place, or thing that evokes an emotional response and related behavior is called attitude.
Sternberg	Sternberg proposed the triarchic theory of intelligence: componential, experiential, and practical. His notion of general intelligence or the g-factor, is a composite of

Go to **Cram101.com** for the Practice Tests for this Chapter.

	intelligence scores across multiple modalities.
Variable	A variable refers to a measurable factor, characteristic, or attribute of an individual or a system.
Adolescence	The period of life bounded by puberty and the assumption of adult responsibilities is adolescence.
Infancy	The developmental period that extends from birth to 18 or 24 months is called infancy.
Kagan	The work of Kagan supports the concept of an inborn, biologically based temperamental predisposition to severe anxiety.
Trait	An enduring personality characteristic that tends to lead to certain behaviors is called a trait. The term trait also means a genetically inherited feature of an organism.
Early childhood	Early childhood refers to the developmental period extending from the end of infancy to about 5 or 6 years of age; sometimes called the preschool years.
Predictive validity	Predictive validity refers to the relation between test scores and the student 's future performance .
Validity	The extent to which a test measures what it is intended to measure is called validity.
Median	The median is a number that separates the higher half of a sample, a population, or a probability distribution from the lower half. It is the middle value in a distribution, above and below which lie an equal number of values.
Pathology	Pathology is the study of the processes underlying disease and other forms of illness, harmful abnormality, or dysfunction.
Construct validity	The extent to which there is evidence that a test measures a particular hypothetical construct is referred to as construct validity.
Control group	A group that does not receive the treatment effect in an experiment is referred to as the control group or sometimes as the comparison group.
Psychometric	Psychometric study is concerned with the theory and technique of psychological measurement, which includes the measurement of knowledge, abilities, attitudes, and personality traits. The field is primarily concerned with the study of differences between individuals
Wechsler Scales	The Wechsler Scales are two well-known intelligence scales, namely the Wechsler Adult Intelligence Scale and the Wechsler Intelligence Scale for Children.
Raw score	A raw score is an original datum that has not been transformed – for example, the original result obtained by a student on a test (i.e., the number of correctly answered items) as opposed to that score after transformation to a standard score or percentile rank or the like.
Cohort	A cohort is a group of individuals defined by their date of birth.
Normative	The term normative is used to describe the effects of those structures of culture which regulate the function of social activity.
Stereotype	A stereotype is considered to be a group concept, held by one social group about another.They are often used in a negative or prejudicial sense and are frequently used to justify certain discriminatory behaviors. This allows powerful social groups to legitimize and protect their dominant position
Survey	A method of scientific investigation in which a large sample of people answer questions about their attitudes or behavior is referred to as a survey.
Baltes	Baltes describes the life-span perspective as one that sees human development as lifelong,

multidimensional, multidirectional, plastic, contextual, and multidisciplinary, and as involving growth, maintenance, and regulation.

Random sample	A sample drawn so that each member of a population has an equal chance of being selected to participate is referred to as a random sample.
Stages	Stages represent relatively discrete periods of time in which functioning is qualitatively different from functioning at other periods.
Society	The social sciences use the term society to mean a group of people that form a semi-closed (or semi-open) social system, in which most interactions are with other individuals belonging to the group.
Individual differences	Individual differences psychology studies the ways in which individual people differ in their behavior. This is distinguished from other aspects of psychology in that although psychology is ostensibly a study of individuals, modern psychologists invariably study groups.
Generalization	In conditioning, the tendency for a conditioned response to be evoked by stimuli that are similar to the stimulus to which the response was conditioned is a generalization. The greater the similarity among the stimuli, the greater the probability of generalization.
Variability	Statistically, variability refers to how much the scores in a distribution spread out, away from the mean.
Primary mental abilities	According to Thurstone, the basic abilities that make up intelligence are called primary mental abilities.
Factor analysis	Factor analysis is a statistical technique that originated in psychometrics. The objective is to explain the most of the variability among a number of observable random variables in terms of a smaller number of unobservable random variables called factors.
Reasoning	Reasoning is the act of using reason to derive a conclusion from certain premises. There are two main methods to reach a conclusion, deductive reasoning and inductive reasoning.
Life span	Life span refers to the upper boundary of life, the maximum number of years an individual can live. The maximum life span of human beings is about 120 years of age. Females live an average of 6 years longer than males.
Hypothesis	A specific statement about behavior or mental processes that is testable through research is a hypothesis.
Task analysis	The procedure of identifying the component elements of a behavior chain is called task analysis.
Pressey	In the early 1920s Pressey developed a machine to provide drill and practice items to students. The teaching machine that Pressey developed resembled a typewriter carriage with a window that revealed a question having four answers.
Social perception	A subfield of social psychology that studies the ways in which we form and modify impressions of others is social perception.
Perception	Perception is the process of acquiring, interpreting, selecting, and organizing sensory information.
Life-span developmental psychology	The study of changes in people as they grow from infancy to old age is referred to as life-span developmental psychology.
Developmental psychology	The branch of psychology that studies the patterns of growth and change occurring throughout life is referred to as developmental psychology.
Norms	In testing, standards of test performance that permit the comparison of one person's score on

the test to the scores of others who have taken the same test are referred to as norms.

Representative sample	Representative sample refers to a sample of participants selected from the larger population in such a way that important subgroups within the population are included in the sample in the same proportions as they are found in the larger population.
Aptitude test	A test designed to predict a person's ability in a particular area or line of work is called an aptitude test.
Cognitive skills	Cognitive skills such as reasoning, attention, and memory can be advanced and sustained through practice and training.
Cultural psychology	Cultural psychology came about in 1960s and 1970s but really became prominent in the 1990's. Contains the idea that culture and mind are inseparable, thus there are no universal laws for how the mind works and that psychological theories grounded in one culture are likely to be limited in applicability when applied to a different culture.
Cronbach	Cronbach is most famous for the development of Cronbach's alpha, a method for determining the reliability of educational and psychological tests. His work on test reliability reached an acme with the creation of generalizability theory, a statistical model for identifying and quantifying the sources of measurement error.
American Psychological Association	The American Psychological Association is a professional organization representing psychology in the US. The mission statement is to "advance psychology as a science and profession and as a means of promoting health, education , and human welfare".
Sullivan	Sullivan developed the Self System, a configuration of the personality traits developed in childhood and reinforced by positive affirmation and the security operations developed in childhood to avoid anxiety and threats to self-esteem.
Emotion	An emotion is a mental states that arise spontaneously, rather than through conscious effort. They are often accompanied by physiological changes.
Adler	Adler argued that human personality could be explained teleologically, separate strands dominated by the guiding purpose of the individual's unconscious self ideal to convert feelings of inferiority to superiority (or rather completeness). The desires of the self ideal were countered by social and ethical demands.
Genetics	Genetics is the science of genes, heredity, and the variation of organisms.
Psychological test	Psychological test refers to a standardized measure of a sample of a person's behavior.
Culture-fair	An intelligence test that does not discriminate against members of any minority group is called culture-fair.
Habit	A habit is a response that has become completely separated from its eliciting stimulus. Early learning theorists used the term to describe S-R associations, however not all S-R associations become a habit, rather many are extinguished after reinforcement is withdrawn.
Subculture	As understood in sociology, anthropology and cultural studies, a subculture is a set of people with a distinct set of behavior and beliefs that differentiate them from a larger culture of which they are a part.
Deprivation	Deprivation, is the loss or withholding of normal stimulation, nutrition, comfort, love, and so forth; a condition of lacking. The level of stimulation is less than what is required.
Senses	The senses are systems that consist of a sensory cell type that respond to a specific kind of physical energy, and that correspond to a defined region within the brain where the signals are received and interpreted.

Go to **Cram101.com** for the Practice Tests for this Chapter.

Cognitive development	The process by which a child's understanding of the world changes as a function of age and experience is called cognitive development.
Aronson	Aronson is credited with refining the theory of cognitive dissonance, which posits that when attitudes and behaviors are inconsistent with one another that psychological discomfort results. This discomfort motivates the person experiencing it to either change their behavior or attitude so that consonance is restored.
Affect	A subjective feeling or emotional tone often accompanied by bodily expressions noticeable to others is called affect.
Verbal intelligence	Verbal intelligence is measured by answering questions involving vocabulary , general information , arithmetic , and other languageor symbol-oriented tasks.
Spatial visualization	An aspect of spatial cognition that involves the mental manipulations of visual stimuli, such as performing mental rotation or solving embedded-figures problems is referred to as spatial visualization.
Cognitive psychology	Cognitive psychology is the psychological science which studies the mental processes that are hypothesised to underlie behavior. This covers a broad range of research domains, examining questions about the workings of memory, attention, perception, knowledge representation, reasoning, creativity and problem solving.
Variance	The degree to which scores differ among individuals in a distribution of scores is the variance.
Empirical	Empirical means the use of working hypotheses which are capable of being disproved using observation or experiment.
Bruner	Bruner has had an enormous impact on educational psychology with his contributions to cognitive learning theory. His ideas are based on categorization, maintaining that people interpret the world in terms of its similarities and differences.
Adaptation	Adaptation is a lowering of sensitivity to a stimulus following prolonged exposure to that stimulus. Behavioral adaptations are special ways a particular organism behaves to survive in its natural habitat.
Psychotherapy	Psychotherapy is a set of techniques based on psychological principles intended to improve mental health, emotional or behavioral issues.
Questionnaire	A self-report method of data collection or clinical assessment method in which the individual being studied checks off items on a printed list, answers multiple-choice questions, or writes out answers to essay questions aimed at producing a selfdescription is called questionnaire.

Personality test	A personality test aims to describe aspects of a person's character that remain stable across situations.
Psychometric	Psychometric study is concerned with the theory and technique of psychological measurement, which includes the measurement of knowledge, abilities, attitudes, and personality traits. The field is primarily concerned with the study of differences between individuals
Personality	Personality refers to the pattern of enduring characteristics that differentiates a person, the patterns of behaviors that make each individual unique.
Factor analysis	Factor analysis is a statistical technique that originated in psychometrics. The objective is to explain the most of the variability among a number of observable random variables in terms of a smaller number of unobservable random variables called factors.
Empirical	Empirical means the use of working hypotheses which are capable of being disproved using observation or experiment.
Personality inventory	A self-report questionnaire by which an examinee indicates whether statements assessing habitual tendencies apply to him or her is referred to as a personality inventory.
Woodworth Personal Data Sheet	The first modern personality test was the Woodworth Personal Data Sheet first used in 1919. It was designed to help the United States Army screen out recruits who might be susceptible to shell shock.
Prototype	A concept of a category of objects or events that serves as a good example of the category is called a prototype.
Psychosomatic	A psychosomatic illness is one with physical manifestations and perhaps a supposed psychological cause. It is often diagnosed when any known or identifiable physical cause was excluded by medical examination.
Compulsion	An apparently irresistible urge to repeat an act or engage in ritualistic behavior such as hand washing is referred to as a compulsion.
Obsession	An obsession is a thought or idea that the sufferer cannot stop thinking about. Common examples include fears of acquiring disease, getting hurt, or causing harm to someone. They are typically automatic, frequent, distressing, and difficult to control or put an end to by themselves.
Nightmare	Nightmare was the original term for the state later known as waking dream, and more currently as sleep paralysis, associated with rapid eye movement (REM) periods of sleep.
Phobia	A persistent, irrational fear of an object, situation, or activity that the person feels compelled to avoid is referred to as a phobia.
Tremor	Tremor is the rhythmic, oscillating shaking movement of the whole body or just a certain part of it, caused by problems of the neurons responsible from muscle action.
Tics	Tics are a repeated, impulsive action, almost reflexive in nature, which the person feels powerless to control or avoid.
Psychopathology	Psychopathology refers to the field concerned with the nature and development of mental disorders.
Norms	In testing, standards of test performance that permit the comparison of one person's score on the test to the scores of others who have taken the same test are referred to as norms.
Psychoticism	Psychoticism is one of the three traits used by the psychologist Hans Eysenck in his P-E-N model of personality. High levels of this trait were believed by Eysenck to be linked to increased vulnerability to psychoses such as schizophrenia.
Depression	In everyday language depression refers to any downturn in mood, which may be relatively

	transitory and perhaps due to something trivial. This is differentiated from Clinical depression which is marked by symptoms that last two weeks or more and are so severe that they interfere with daily living.
Paranoid	The term paranoid is typically used in a general sense to signify any self-referential delusion, or more specifically, to signify a delusion involving the fear of persecution.
Anxiety	Anxiety is a complex combination of the feeling of fear, apprehension and worry often accompanied by physical sensations such as palpitations, chest pain and/or shortness of breath.
Questionnaire	A self-report method of data collection or clinical assessment method in which the individual being studied checks off items on a printed list, answers multiple-choice questions, or writes out answers to essay questions aimed at producing a selfdescription is called questionnaire.
Perception	Perception is the process of acquiring, interpreting, selecting, and organizing sensory information.
Hypothesis	A specific statement about behavior or mental processes that is testable through research is a hypothesis.
Validity	The extent to which a test measures what it is intended to measure is called validity.
Minnesota Multiphasic Personality Inventory	The Minnesota Multiphasic Personality Inventory is the most frequently used test in the mental health fields. This assessment or test helps identify personal, social, and behavioral problems in psychiatric patients. This test helps provide relevant information to aid in problem identification, diagnosis, and treatment planning for the patient.
Graham	Graham has conducted a number of studies that reveal stronger socioeconomic-status influences rather than ethnic influences in achievement.
Clinical psychologist	A psychologist, usually with a Ph.D, whose training is in the diagnosis, treatment, or research of psychological and behavioral disorders is a clinical psychologist.
Population	Population refers to all members of a well-defined group of organisms, events, or things.
Normative	The term normative is used to describe the effects of those structures of culture which regulate the function of social activity.
Psychotic behavior	A psychotic behavior is a severe psychological disorder characterized by hallucinations and loss of contact with reality.
Ideas of reference	Ideas of reference involve a person having a belief or perception that irrelevant, unrelated or innocuous things in the world are referring to them directly or have special personal significance.
Hallucination	A hallucination is a sensory perception experienced in the absence of an external stimulus, as distinct from an illusion, which is a misperception of an external stimulus. They may occur in any sensory modality - visual, auditory, olfactory, gustatory, tactile, or mixed.
Affective	Affective is the way people react emotionally, their ability to feel another living thing's pain or joy.
Delusion	A false belief, not generally shared by others, and that cannot be changed despite strong evidence to the contrary is a delusion.
Attitude	An enduring mental representation of a person, place, or thing that evokes an emotional response and related behavior is called attitude.
Control group	A group that does not receive the treatment effect in an experiment is referred to as the control group or sometimes as the comparison group.

Go to **Cram101.com** for the Practice Tests for this Chapter.

Introversion	A personality trait characterized by intense imagination and a tendency to inhibit impulses is called introversion.
Masculinity	Masculinity is a culturally determined value reflecting the set of characteristics of maleness.
Homosexual	Homosexual refers to a sexual orientation characterized by aesthetic attraction, romantic love, and sexual desire exclusively for members of the same sex or gender identity.
Femininity	Femininity is the set of characteristics defined by a culture for idealized females.
Stereotype	A stereotype is considered to be a group concept, held by one social group about another. They are often used in a negative or prejudicial sense and are frequently used to justify certain discriminatory behaviors. This allows powerful social groups to legitimize and protect their dominant position
Extraversion	Extraversion, one of the big-five personailty traits, is marked by pronounced engagement with the external world. They are people who enjoy being with people, are full of energy, and often experience positive emotions.
Response set	A tendency to answer test items according to a personal or situational bias is called response set.
Malingering	Malingering is a medical and psychological term that refers to an individual faking the symptoms of mental or physical disorders for a myriad of reasons such as fraud, dereliction of responsibilities, attempting to obtain medications or to lighten criminal sentences.
Variable	A variable refers to a measurable factor, characteristic, or attribute of an individual or a system.
Ego	In Freud's view the Ego serves to balance our primitive needs and our moral beliefs and taboos. Relying on experience, a healthy Ego provides the ability to adapt to reality and interact with the outside world.
Demographic variable	A varying characteristic that is a vital or social statistic of an individual, sample group, or population, for example, age, sex, socioeconomic status, racial origin, education is called a demographic variable.
Ethnicity	Ethnicity refers to a characteristic based on cultural heritage, nationality characteristics, race, religion, and language.
Raw score	A raw score is an original datum that has not been transformed – for example, the original result obtained by a student on a test (i.e., the number of correctly answered items) as opposed to that score after transformation to a standard score or percentile rank or the like.
Empiricism	Empiricism is generally regarded as being at the heart of the modern scientific method, that our theories should be based on our observations of the world rather than on intuition, or deductive logic.
Stages	Stages represent relatively discrete periods of time in which functioning is qualitatively different from functioning at other periods.
Adaptation	Adaptation is a lowering of sensitivity to a stimulus following prolonged exposure to that stimulus. Behavioral adaptations are special ways a particular organism behaves to survive in its natural habitat.
California Psychological Inventory	A highly regarded personality test used to assess personality, the California Psychological Inventory is a standardized test in which individuals respond to a large number of items that reflect a number of traits and respond by saying whether the items are like them or not like them.

101

113

Socialization	Social rules and social relations are created, communicated, and changed in verbal and nonverbal ways creating social complexity useful in identifying outsiders and intelligent breeding partners. The process of learning these skills is called socialization.
Empathy	Empathy is the recognition and understanding of the states of mind, including beliefs, desires and particularly emotions of others without injecting your own.
Trait	An enduring personality characteristic that tends to lead to certain behaviors is called a trait. The term trait also means a genetically inherited feature of an organism.
Correlation	A statistical technique for determining the degree of association between two or more variables is referred to as correlation.
Socioeconomic	Socioeconomic pertains to the study of the social and economic impacts of any product or service offering, market intervention or other activity on an economy as a whole and on the companies, organization and individuals who are its main economic actors.
Cross-cultural studies	Cross-cultural studies are comparisons of a culture with one or more other cultures, which provides information about the degree to which behavior is similar across cultures or the degree to which it is culture specific .
Ethnic group	An ethnic group is a culture or subculture whose members are readily distinguishable by outsiders based on traits originating from a common racial, national, linguistic, or religious source. Members of an ethnic group are often presumed to be culturally or biologically similar, although this is not in fact necessarily the case.
Personality type	A persistent style of complex behaviors defined by a group of related traits is referred to as a personality type. Myer Friedman and his co-workers first defined personality types in the 1950s. Friedman classified people into 2 categories, Type A and Type B.
Cognitive development	The process by which a child's understanding of the world changes as a function of age and experience is called cognitive development.
Hyperactivity	Hyperactivity can be described as a state in which a individual is abnormally easily excitable and exuberant. Strong emotional reactions and a very short span of attention is also typical for the individual.
Construct	A generalized concept, such as anxiety or gravity, is a construct.
Heterogeneous	A heterogeneous compound, mixture, or other such object is one that consists of many different items, which are often not easily sorted or separated, though they are clearly distinct.
Personality trait	According to the Diagnostic and Statistical Manual of the American Psychiatric Association, a personality trait is a "prominent aspect of personality that is exhibited in a wide range of important social and personal contexts. ...".
Guilford	Guilford observed that most individuals display a preference for either convergent or divergent thinking. Scientists and engineers typically prefer the former and artists and performers, the latter.
Temperament	Temperament refers to a basic, innate disposition to change behavior. The activity level is an important dimension of temperament.
Survey	A method of scientific investigation in which a large sample of people answer questions about their attitudes or behavior is referred to as a survey.
Allport	Allport was a trait theorist. Those traits he believed to predominate a person's personality were called central traits. Traits such that one could be indentifed by the trait, were referred to as cardinal traits. Central traits and cardinal traits are influenced by environmental factors.

115

Source traits	Cattell's name for the traits that make up the most basic personality structure and causes of behavior is source traits.
Consciousness	The awareness of the sensations, thoughts, and feelings being experienced at a given moment is called consciousness.
Problem solving	An attempt to find an appropriate way of attaining a goal when the goal is not readily available is called problem solving.
Reasoning	Reasoning is the act of using reason to derive a conclusion from certain premises. There are two main methods to reach a conclusion, deductive reasoning and inductive reasoning.
Test-retest reliability	The consistency of a measure when it is repeated over time is called test-retest reliability. It involves administering the test to the same group of people at least twice. The first set of scores is correlated with the second set of scores. Correlations range between 0 (low reliability) and 1 (high reliability).
Reliability	Reliability means the extent to which a test produces a consistent , reproducible score .
Five-factor model	The five-factor model of personality proposes that there are five universal dimensions of personality: Neuroticism, Extraversion, Openness, Conscientiousness, and Agreeableness.
Attention	Attention is the cognitive process of selectively concentrating on one thing while ignoring other things. Psychologists have labeled three types of attention: sustained attention, selective attention, and divided attention.
Openness to Experience	Openness to Experience, one of the big-five traits, describes a dimension of cognitive style that distinguishes imaginative, creative people from down-to-earth, conventional people.
Neuroticism	Eysenck's use of the term neuroticism (or Emotional Stability) was proposed as the dimension describing individual differences in the predisposition towards neurotic disorder.
Big five	The big five factors of personality are Openness to experience, Conscientiousness, Extraversion, Agreeableness, and Emotional Stability.
Theories	Theories are logically self-consistent models or frameworks describing the behavior of a certain natural or social phenomenon. They are broad explanations and predictions concerning phenomena of interest.
Millon Clinical Multiaxial Inventory	The Millon Clinical Multiaxial Inventory is a self-report assessment of personality disorders and clinical syndromes. This is sometimes used as an adjunct instrument in comprehensive neuropsychological assessment.
Syndrome	The term syndrome is the association of several clinically recognizable features, signs, symptoms, phenomena or characteristics which often occur together, so that the presence of one feature indicates the presence of the others.
Pathology	Pathology is the study of the processes underlying disease and other forms of illness, harmful abnormality, or dysfunction.
Clinical assessment	A clinical assessment is a systematic evaluation and measurement of psychological, biological, and social factors in a person presenting with a possible psychological disorder.
Jung	Jung was in some aspects a response to Sigmund Freud's psychoanalysis. He proposed and developed the concepts of the extroverted and introverted personality, archetypes, and the collective unconscious. His work has been influential in psychiatry and in the study of religion, literature, and related fields.
Construct validity	The extent to which there is evidence that a test measures a particular hypothetical construct is referred to as construct validity.
Sensation	Sensation is the first stage in the chain of biochemical and neurologic events that begins

Go to **Cram101.com** for the Practice Tests for this Chapter.

101

117

with the impinging of a stimulus upon the receptor cells of a sensory organ, which then leads to perception, the mental state that is reflected in statements like "I see a uniformly blue wall."

Guthrie	The theory of learning proposed by Guthrie was based on one principle, Contiguity : A combination of stimuli which has accompanied a movement will on its recurrence tend to be followed by that movement. Prediction of behavior will always be probabilistic.
Agreeableness	Agreeableness, one of the big-five personality traits, reflects individual differences in concern with cooperation and social harmony. It is the degree individuals value getting along with others.
Response bias	Response bias is a type of statistical bias which can affect the results of a statistical survey if respondents answer questions in the way they think the questioner wants them to answer rather than according to their true beliefs.
Self-report inventories	Personality tests that ask individuals to answer a series of questions about their own characteristic behaviors are called self-report inventories.
Face validity	Condition of testing in which test items appear plausible for their intended purposes is called face validity.
Simulation	A simulation is an imitation of some real device or state of affairs. Simulation attempts to represent certain features of the behavior of a physical or abstract system by the behavior of another system.
Psychotherapy	Psychotherapy is a set of techniques based on psychological principles intended to improve mental health, emotional or behavioral issues.
Impression management	Impression management is the process through which people try to control the impressions other people form of them.
Reid	Reid was the founder of the Scottish School of Common Sense, and played an integral role in the Scottish Enlightenment. He advocated direct realism, or common sense realism, and argued strongly against the Theory of Ideas advocated by John Locke and René Descartes.
Defense mechanism	A Defense mechanism is a set of unconscious ways to protect one's personality from unpleasant thoughts and realities which may otherwise cause anxiety. The notion is an integral part of the psychoanalytic theory.
Psychoanalytic	Freud's theory that unconscious forces act as determinants of personality is called psychoanalytic theory. The theory is a developmental theory characterized by critical stages of development.
Self-esteem	Self-esteem refers to a person's subjective appraisal of himself or herself as intrinsically positive or negative to some degree.
Self-image	A person's self-image is the mental picture, generally of a kind that is quite resistant to change, that depicts not only details that are potentially available to objective investigation by others, but also items that have been learned by that person about himself or herself.
Forced-choice format	A method of presenting test questions that requires a respondent to select one of a number of possible answers is a forced-choice format.
Variance	The degree to which scores differ among individuals in a distribution of scores is the variance.
Generalizability	The ability to extend a set of findings observed in one piece of research to other situations and groups is called generalizability.

Go to **Cram101.com** for the Practice Tests for this Chapter.

119

Learning	Learning is a relatively permanent change in behavior that results from experience. Thus, to attribute a behavioral change to learning, the change must be relatively permanent and must result from experience.
Behavior modification	Behavior Modification is a technique of altering an individual's reactions to stimuli through positive reinforcement and the extinction of maladaptive behavior.
Cognitive theories	Cognitive theories emphasize thinking, reasoning, problem solving, and language. Contributions include an emphasis on the active construction of understanding and developmental changes in thinking. Criticisms include giving too little attention to individual variations and underrating the unconscious aspects of thought.
Behavior therapy	Behavior therapy refers to the systematic application of the principles of learning to direct modification of a client's problem behaviors.
Social learning	Social learning is learning that occurs as a function of observing, retaining and replicating behavior observed in others. Although social learning can occur at any stage in life, it is thought to be particularly important during childhood, particularly as authority becomes important.
Bandura	Bandura is best known for his work on social learning theory or Social Cognitivism. His famous Bobo doll experiment illustrated that people learn from observing others.
Mischel	Mischel is known for his cognitive social learning model of personality that focuses on the specific cognitive variables that mediate the manner in which new experiences affect the individual.
Cognitive skills	Cognitive skills such as reasoning, attention, and memory can be advanced and sustained through practice and training.
Individual traits	Personality traits that define a person's unique individual qualities are called individual traits.
Heredity	Heredity is the transfer of characteristics from parent to offspring through their genes.
Research design	A research design tests a hypothesis. The basic typess are: descriptive, correlational, and experimental.
Individual differences	Individual differences psychology studies the ways in which individual people differ in their behavior. This is distinguished from other aspects of psychology in that although psychology is ostensibly a study of individuals, modern psychologists invariably study groups.
Random sample	A sample drawn so that each member of a population has an equal chance of being selected to participate is referred to as a random sample.
Moderator variable	A variable that affects the relation between two other variables is called the moderator variable.
Intrapersonal	Intrapersonal is the ability to recognize, define, and pursue inner feelings and thoughts, as in poetry and self-knowledge.
Threshold	In general, a threshold is a fixed location or value where an abrupt change is observed. In the sensory modalities, it is the minimum amount of stimulus energy necessary to elicit a sensory response.
Premise	A premise is a statement presumed true within the context of a discourse, especially of a logical argument.
Idiographic	An idiographic investigation studies the characteristics of an individual in depth.
Ecological psychology	Ecological psychology emphasises real world studies of behavior as opposed to the artificial environment of the laboratory.

Go to **Cram101.com** for the Practice Tests for this Chapter.

121

Roger Barker	In his classic work "Ecological Psychology" (1968), Roger Barker argued that human behavior was radically situated: in other words, you couldn't make predictions about human behavior unless you know what situation or context or environment the human in question was in.
Variability	Statistically, variability refers to how much the scores in a distribution spread out, away from the mean.
Social role	Social role refers to expected behavior patterns associated with particular social positions.
Test anxiety	High levels of arousal and worry that seriously impair test performance is referred to as test anxiety.
Psychological testing	Psychological testing is a field characterized by the use of small samples of behavior in order to infer larger generalizations about a given individual. The technical term for psychological testing is psychometrics.
Acute	Acute means sudden, sharp, and abrupt. Usually short in duration.
Test reliability	Test Reliability is the extent to which a test is repeatable and yields consistent scores.
Resurgence	Resurgence refers to the reappearance during extinction, of a previously reinforced behavior.

123

Personality	Personality refers to the pattern of enduring characteristics that differentiates a person, the patterns of behaviors that make each individual unique.
Attitude	An enduring mental representation of a person, place, or thing that evokes an emotional response and related behavior is called attitude.
Variable	A variable refers to a measurable factor, characteristic, or attribute of an individual or a system.
Social psychologists	Social psychologists study the nature and causes of human social behavior, emphasizing on how people think and relate towards each other.
Social psychology	Social psychology is the study of the nature and causes of human social behavior, with an emphasis on how people think towards each other and how they relate to each other.
Allport	Allport was a trait theorist. Those traits he believed to predominate a person's personality were called central traits. Traits such that one could be indentifed by the trait, were referred to as cardinal traits. Central traits and cardinal traits are influenced by environmental factors.
Attention	Attention is the cognitive process of selectively concentrating on one thing while ignoring other things. Psychologists have labeled three types of attention: sustained attention, selective attention, and divided attention.
Empirical	Empirical means the use of working hypotheses which are capable of being disproved using observation or experiment.
Socialization	Social rules and social relations are created, communicated, and changed in verbal and nonverbal ways creating social complexity useful in identifying outsiders and intelligent breeding partners. The process of learning these skills is called socialization.
Norms	In testing, standards of test performance that permit the comparison of one person's score on the test to the scores of others who have taken the same test are referred to as norms.
Population	Population refers to all members of a well-defined group of organisms, events, or things.
Psychometric	Psychometric study is concerned with the theory and technique of psychological measurement, which includes the measurement of knowledge, abilities, attitudes, and personality traits. The field is primarily concerned with the study of differences between individuals
Validity	The extent to which a test measures what it is intended to measure is called validity.
Learning	Learning is a relatively permanent change in behavior that results from experience. Thus, to attribute a behavioral change to learning, the change must be relatively permanent and must result from experience.
Statistics	Statistics is a type of data analysis which practice includes the planning, summarizing, and interpreting of observations of a system possibly followed by predicting or forecasting of future events based on a mathematical model of the system being observed.
Statistic	A statistic is an observable random variable of a sample.
Correlation	A statistical technique for determining the degree of association between two or more variables is referred to as correlation.
Heterogeneous	A heterogeneous compound, mixture, or other such object is one that consists of many different items, which are often not easily sorted or separated, though they are clearly distinct.
Homogeneous	In biology homogeneous has a meaning similar to its meaning in mathematics. Generally it means "the same" or "of the same quality or general property".

125

Factor analysis	Factor analysis is a statistical technique that originated in psychometrics. The objective is to explain the most of the variability among a number of observable random variables in terms of a smaller number of unobservable random variables called factors.
Raw score	A raw score is an original datum that has not been transformed – for example, the original result obtained by a student on a test (i.e., the number of correctly answered items) as opposed to that score after transformation to a standard score or percentile rank or the like.
Normative	The term normative is used to describe the effects of those structures of culture which regulate the function of social activity.
Counselor	A counselor is a mental health professional who specializes in helping people with problems not involving serious mental disorders.
Reliability	Reliability means the extent to which a test produces a consistent , reproducible score .
Median	The median is a number that separates the higher half of a sample, a population, or a probability distribution from the lower half. It is the middle value in a distribution, above and below which lie an equal number of values.
Predictive validity	Predictive validity refers to the relation between test scores and the student 's future performance .
Construct	A generalized concept, such as anxiety or gravity, is a construct.
Heuristic	A heuristic is a simple, efficient rule of thumb proposed to explain how people make decisions, come to judgments and solve problems, typically when facing complex problems or incomplete information. These rules work well under most circumstances, but in certain cases lead to systematic cognitive biases.
Scheme	According to Piaget, a hypothetical mental structure that permits the classification and organization of new information is called a scheme.
Counseling psychologist	A doctoral level mental health professional whose training is similar to that of a clinical psychologist, though usually with less emphasis on research and serious psychopathology is referred to as a counseling psychologist.
Survey	A method of scientific investigation in which a large sample of people answer questions about their attitudes or behavior is referred to as a survey.
Response bias	Response bias is a type of statistical bias which can affect the results of a statistical survey if respondents answer questions in the way they think the questioner wants them to answer rather than according to their true beliefs.
Forced-choice format	A method of presenting test questions that requires a respondent to select one of a number of possible answers is a forced-choice format.
Content validity	The degree to which the content of a test is representative of the domain it's supposed to cover is referred to as its content validity.
Percentile score	A figure that indicates the percentage of people who score below the score the individual of interest has obtained, is called the percentile score.
Transposition	When a principle learned in one problem-solving situation is applied to the solution of another problem, the process is referred to as transposition.
Concurrent validity	Concurrent validity is demonstrated where a test correlates well with a measure that has previously been validated.
Self-concept	Self-concept refers to domain-specific evaluations of the self where a domain may be academics, athletics, etc.

Go to **Cram101.com** for the Practice Tests for this Chapter.

Overgenerali-ation	Overgeneralization is concluding that all instances of some kind of event will turn out a certain way because one or more in the past did. For instance, a class goes badly one day and I conclude, "I'll never be a good teacher."
Self-understanding	Self-understanding is a child's cognitive representation of the self, the substance and content of the child's self-conceptions.
Cognitive psychology	Cognitive psychology is the psychological science which studies the mental processes that are hypothesised to underlie behavior. This covers a broad range of research domains, examining questions about the workings of memory, attention, perception, knowledge representation, reasoning, creativity and problem solving.
Paradigm	Paradigm refers to the set of practices that defines a scientific discipline during a particular period of time. It provides a framework from which to conduct research, it ensures that a certain range of phenomena, those on which the paradigm focuses, are explored thoroughly. Itmay also blind scientists to other, perhaps more fruitful, ways of dealing with their subject matter.
Insight	Insight refers to a sudden awareness of the relationships among various elements that had previously appeared to be independent of one another.
Reinforcer	In operant conditioning, a reinforcer is any stimulus that increases the probability that a preceding behavior will occur again. In Classical Conditioning, the unconditioned stimulus (US) is the reinforcer.
Attitude scale	A multiple-item questionnaire designed to measure a person's attitude toward some object is called an attitude scale.
Overt behavior	An action or response that is directly observable and measurable is an overt behavior.
Stimulus	A change in an environmental condition that elicits a response is a stimulus.
Job satisfaction	A person's attitudes and feelings about his or her job and facets of the job is called job satisfaction.
Ethnic group	An ethnic group is a culture or subculture whose members are readily distinguishable by outsiders based on traits originating from a common racial, national, linguistic, or religious source. Members of an ethnic group are often presumed to be culturally or biologically similar, although this is not in fact necessarily the case.
Punishment	Punishment is the addtion of a stimulus that reduces the frequency of a response, or the removal of a stimulus that results in a reduction of the response.
Adaptation	Adaptation is a lowering of sensitivity to a stimulus following prolonged exposure to that stimulus. Behavioral adaptations are special ways a particular organism behaves to survive in its natural habitat.
Thurstone	Thurstone was a pioneer in the field of psychometrics. His work in factor analysis led him to formulate a model of intelligence center around "Primary Mental Abilities", which were independent group factors of intelligence that different individuals possessed in varying degrees.
Variability	Statistically, variability refers to how much the scores in a distribution spread out, away from the mean.
Guttman scale	The Guttman scale is a comparative scaling technique. It proposes that those who agree with a more extreme test item will also agree with all less extreme items that preceded it.
Likert scale	A Likert scale is a type of psychometric scale often used in questionnaires. It asks respondents to specify their level of agreement to each of a list of statements. It is a bipolar scaling method, measuring either positive and negative response to a statement.

Go to **Cram101.com** for the Practice Tests for this Chapter.

129

Locus of control	The place to which an individual attributes control over the receiving of reinforcers -either inside or outside the self is referred to as locus of control.
Self-esteem	Self-esteem refers to a person's subjective appraisal of himself or herself as intrinsically positive or negative to some degree.
Individual differences	Individual differences psychology studies the ways in which individual people differ in their behavior. This is distinguished from other aspects of psychology in that although psychology is ostensibly a study of individuals, modern psychologists invariably study groups.
Masculinity	Masculinity is a culturally determined value reflecting the set of characteristics of maleness.
Reinforcement	In operant conditioning, reinforcement is any change in an environment that (a) occurs after the behavior, (b) seems to make that behavior re-occur more often in the future and (c) that reoccurence of behavior must be the result of the change.
Rotter	Rotter focused on the application of social learning theory (SLT) to clinical psychology. She introduced the ideas of learning from generalized expectancies of reinforcement and internal/external locus of control (self-initiated change versus change influenced by others). According to Rotter, health outcomes could be improved by the development of a sense of personal control over one's life.
Perception	Perception is the process of acquiring, interpreting, selecting, and organizing sensory information.
Negative reinforcement	During negative reinforcement, a stimulus is removed and the frequency of the behavior or response increases.
Construct validity	The extent to which there is evidence that a test measures a particular hypothetical construct is referred to as construct validity.
Variance	The degree to which scores differ among individuals in a distribution of scores is the variance.
Questionnaire	A self-report method of data collection or clinical assessment method in which the individual being studied checks off items on a printed list, answers multiple-choice questions, or writes out answers to essay questions aimed at producing a selfdescription is called questionnaire.
Society	The social sciences use the term society to mean a group of people that form a semi-closed (or semi-open) social system, in which most interactions are with other individuals belonging to the group.
Affect	A subjective feeling or emotional tone often accompanied by bodily expressions noticeable to others is called affect.

131

Psychometric	Psychometric study is concerned with the theory and technique of psychological measurement, which includes the measurement of knowledge, abilities, attitudes, and personality traits. The field is primarily concerned with the study of differences between individuals
Personality	Personality refers to the pattern of enduring characteristics that differentiates a person, the patterns of behaviors that make each individual unique.
Rorschach	The Rorschach inkblot test is a method of psychological evaluation. It is a projective test associated with the Freudian school of thought. Psychologists use this test to try to probe the unconscious minds of their patients.
Hypothesis	A specific statement about behavior or mental processes that is testable through research is a hypothesis.
Attention	Attention is the cognitive process of selectively concentrating on one thing while ignoring other things. Psychologists have labeled three types of attention: sustained attention, selective attention, and divided attention.
Trait	An enduring personality characteristic that tends to lead to certain behaviors is called a trait. The term trait also means a genetically inherited feature of an organism.
Clinician	A health professional authorized to provide services to people suffering from one or more pathologies is a clinician.
Art therapy	Art therapy is a type of psychotherapy based upon the assumption that with an engagement in life-enhancing creative processes and the analyses of these processes, individuals will increase awareness and empathy with external reality and within one's self. They will improve skills to cope with symptoms, experiences and trauma, and enhance cognitive abilities.
Psychoanalytic	Freud's theory that unconscious forces act as determinants of personality is called psychoanalytic theory. The theory is a developmental theory characterized by critical stages of development.
Stimulus	A change in an environmental condition that elicits a response is a stimulus.
Theories	Theories are logically self-consistent models or frameworks describing the behavior of a certain natural or social phenomenon. They are broad explanations and predictions concerning phenomena of interest.
Postulates	Postulates are general statements about behavior that cannot be directly verified. They are used to generate theorems which can be tested.
Reaction time	The amount of time required to respond to a stimulus is referred to as reaction time.
Quantitative	A quantitative property is one that exists in a range of magnitudes, and can therefore be measured. Measurements of any particular quantitative property are expressed as as a specific quantity, referred to as a unit, multiplied by a number.
Evolution	Commonly used to refer to gradual change, evolution is the change in the frequency of alleles within a population from one generation to the next. This change may be caused by different mechanisms, including natural selection, genetic drift, or changes in population (gene flow).
Perception	Perception is the process of acquiring, interpreting, selecting, and organizing sensory information.
Psychopathology	Psychopathology refers to the field concerned with the nature and development of mental disorders.
Interdependence	Interdependence is a dynamic of being mutually responsible to and dependent on others.
Variability	Statistically, variability refers to how much the scores in a distribution spread out, away from the mean.

Go to **Cram101.com** for the Practice Tests for this Chapter.

Clinical psychologist	A psychologist, usually with a Ph.D, whose training is in the diagnosis, treatment, or research of psychological and behavioral disorders is a clinical psychologist.
Variable	A variable refers to a measurable factor, characteristic, or attribute of an individual or a system.
Reliability	Reliability means the extent to which a test produces a consistent , reproducible score .
Validity	The extent to which a test measures what it is intended to measure is called validity.
Convergent validity	Convergent validity measures whether a test returns similar results to other tests which purport to measure the same or related constructs.
Construct	A generalized concept, such as anxiety or gravity, is a construct.
Psychoanalytic theory	Psychoanalytic theory is a general term for approaches to psychoanalysis which attempt to provide a conceptual framework more-or-less independent of clinical practice rather than based on empirical analysis of clinical cases.
Psychodynamic	Most psychodynamic approaches are centered around the idea of a maladapted function developed early in life (usually childhood) which are at least in part unconscious. This maladapted function (a.k.a. defense mechanism) does not do well in place of a normal/healthy one.
Adaptation	Adaptation is a lowering of sensitivity to a stimulus following prolonged exposure to that stimulus. Behavioral adaptations are special ways a particular organism behaves to survive in its natural habitat.
Psychological test	Psychological test refers to a standardized measure of a sample of a person's behavior.
Resurgence	Resurgence refers to the reappearance during extinction, of a previously reinforced behavior.
Affective	Affective is the way people react emotionally, their ability to feel another living thing's pain or joy.
Empirical	Empirical means the use of working hypotheses which are capable of being disproved using observation or experiment.
Anxiety	Anxiety is a complex combination of the feeling of fear, apprehension and worry often accompanied by physical sensations such as palpitations, chest pain and/or shortness of breath.
Test-retest reliability	The consistency of a measure when it is repeated over time is called test-retest reliability. It involves administering the test to the same group of people at least twice. The first set of scores is correlated with the second set of scores. Correlations range between 0 (low reliability) and 1 (high reliability).
Correlation	A statistical technique for determining the degree of association between two or more variables is referred to as correlation.
Thematic Apperception Test	The Thematic Apperception Test uses a standard series of provocative yet ambiguous pictures about which the subject must tell a story. Each story is carefully analyzed to uncover underlying needs, attitudes, and patterns of reaction.
Construct validity	The extent to which there is evidence that a test measures a particular hypothetical construct is referred to as construct validity.
Apperception	A newly experienced sensation is related to past experiences to form an understood situation. For Wundt, consciousness is composed of two "stages:" There is a large capacity working memory called the Blickfeld and the narrower consciousness called Apperception, or selective attention.

Go to **Cram101.com** for the Practice Tests for this Chapter.

Normative	The term normative is used to describe the effects of those structures of culture which regulate the function of social activity.
Norms	In testing, standards of test performance that permit the comparison of one person's score on the test to the scores of others who have taken the same test are referred to as norms.
Scheme	According to Piaget, a hypothetical mental structure that permits the classification and organization of new information is called a scheme.
Rubric	In education, a rubric is a set of criteria and standards linked to learning objectives that is used to assess a student's performance on a paper, project, essay, etc.
Projective hypothesis	The projective hypothesis suggests that highly unstructured stimuli, as in the Rorschach Test, are necessary to bypass an individual's defenses in order to reveal unconscious motives and conflicts.
Deprivation	Deprivation, is the loss or withholding of normal stimulation, nutrition, comfort, love, and so forth; a condition of lacking. The level of stimulation is less than what is required.
Affect	A subjective feeling or emotional tone often accompanied by bodily expressions noticeable to others is called affect.
Clinical assessment	A clinical assessment is a systematic evaluation and measurement of psychological, biological, and social factors in a person presenting with a possible psychological disorder.
Defense mechanism	A Defense mechanism is a set of unconscious ways to protect one's personality from unpleasant thoughts and realities which may otherwise cause anxiety. The notion is an integral part of the psychoanalytic theory.
Object relation	Object relation theory is the idea that the ego-self exists only in relation to other objects, which may be external or internal.
Attitude	An enduring mental representation of a person, place, or thing that evokes an emotional response and related behavior is called attitude.
Ethnic group	An ethnic group is a culture or subculture whose members are readily distinguishable by outsiders based on traits originating from a common racial, national, linguistic, or religious source. Members of an ethnic group are often presumed to be culturally or biologically similar, although this is not in fact necessarily the case.
Population	Population refers to all members of a well-defined group of organisms, events, or things.
McClelland	McClelland asserts that human motivation comprises three dominant needs: the need for achievement (N-Ach), the need for power (N-Pow) and the need for affiliation (N-Affil). The subjective importance of each need varies from individual to individual and depends also on an individual's cultural background.
Questionnaire	A self-report method of data collection or clinical assessment method in which the individual being studied checks off items on a printed list, answers multiple-choice questions, or writes out answers to essay questions aimed at producing a selfdescription is called questionnaire.
Motivation	In psychology, motivation is the driving force (desire) behind all actions of an organism.
Ideology	An ideology can be thought of as a comprehensive vision, as a way of looking at things, as in common sense and several philosophical tendencies, or a set of ideas proposed by the dominant class of a society to all members of this society.
Motives	Needs or desires that energize and direct behavior toward a goal are motives.
Standardized test	An oral or written assessment for which an individual receives a score indicating how the individual reponded relative to a previously tested large sample of others is referred to as

	a standardized test.
Stereotype	A stereotype is considered to be a group concept, held by one social group about another. They are often used in a negative or prejudicial sense and are frequently used to justify certain discriminatory behaviors. This allows powerful social groups to legitimize and protect their dominant position
Ego	In Freud's view the Ego serves to balance our primitive needs and our moral beliefs and taboos. Relying on experience, a healthy Ego provides the ability to adapt to reality and interact with the outside world.
Conformity	Conformity is the degree to which members of a group will change their behavior, views and attitudes to fit the views of the group. The group can influence members via unconscious processes or via overt social pressure on individuals.
Projective test	A projective test is a personality test designed to let a person respond to ambiguous stimuli, presumably revealing hidden emotions and internal conflicts. This is different from an "objective test" in which responses are analyzed according to a universal standard rather than an individual psychiatrist's judgement.
Free association	In psychoanalysis, the uncensored uttering of all thoughts that come to mind is called free association.
Galton	Galton was one of the first experimental psychologists, and the founder of the field of Differential Psychology, which concerns itself with individual differences rather than on common trends. He created the statistical methods correlation and regression.
Wundt	Wundt, considered the father of experimental psychology, created the first laboratory in psychology in 1879. His methodology was based on introspection and his body of work founded the school of thought called Voluntarism.
Psychiatrist	A psychiatrist is a physician who specializes in the diagnosis and treatment of psychological disorders.
Kraepelin	Kraepelin postulated that there is a specific brain or other biological pathology underlying each of the major psychiatric disorders. Just as his laboratory discovered the pathologic basis of what is now known as Alzheimers disease, Kraepelin was confident that it would someday be possible to identify the pathologic basis of each of the major psychiatric disorders.
Psychoanalyst	A psychoanalyst is a specially trained therapist who attempts to treat the individual by uncovering and revealing to the individual otherwise subconscious factors that are contributing to some undesirable behavor.
Jung	Jung was in some aspects a response to Sigmund Freud's psychoanalysis. He proposed and developed the concepts of the extroverted and introverted personality, archetypes, and the collective unconscious. His work has been influential in psychiatry and in the study of religion, literature, and related fields.
Socioeconomic	Socioeconomic pertains to the study of the social and economic impacts of any product or service offering, market intervention or other activity on an economy as a whole and on the companies, organization and individuals who are its main economic actors.
Creativity	Creativity is the ability to think about something in novel and unusual ways and come up with unique solutions to problems. It involves divergent thinking, having many solutions or views to a problem.
Verbal Behavior	Verbal Behavior is a book written by B.F. Skinner in which the author presents his ideas on language. For Skinner, speech, along with other forms of communication, was simply a behavior. Skinner argued that each act of speech is an inevitable consequence of the

	speaker's current environment and his behavioral and sensory history.
Rotter	Rotter focused on the application of social learning theory (SLT) to clinical psychology. She introduced the ideas of learning from generalized expectancies of reinforcement and internal/external locus of control (self-initiated change versus change influenced by others). According to Rotter, health outcomes could be improved by the development of a sense of personal control over one's life.
Maladjustment	Maladjustment is the condition of being unable to adapt properly to your environment with resulting emotional instability.
Malingering	Malingering is a medical and psychological term that refers to an individual faking the symptoms of mental or physical disorders for a myriad of reasons such as fraud, dereliction of responsibilities, attempting to obtain medications or to lighten criminal sentences.
Psychodynamic psychotherapy	The "goal" of psychodynamic therapy is the experience of "truth." This "truth" must be encountered through the breakdown of psychological defenses. Psychodynamic psychotherapy involves a great idea of introspection and reflection from the client.
Individual psychology	Alfred Adler's individual psychology approach views people as motivated by purposes and goals, being creators of their own lives .
Psychotherapy	Psychotherapy is a set of techniques based on psychological principles intended to improve mental health, emotional or behavioral issues.
Adler	Adler argued that human personality could be explained teleologically, separate strands dominated by the guiding purpose of the individual's unconscious self ideal to convert feelings of inferiority to superiority (or rather completeness). The desires of the self ideal were countered by social and ethical demands.
Autobiograph-cal memory	An Autobiographical Memory is a personal representation of general or specific events and personal facts.
Metaphor	A metaphor is a rhetorical trope where a comparison is made between two seemingly unrelated subjects
Empirical evidence	Facts or information based on direct observation or experience are referred to as empirical evidence.
Multiple regression	A multiple regression is a linear regression with more than one covariate (predictor variable). It can be viewed as a simple case of canonical correlation.
Regression	Return to a form of behavior characteristic of an earlier stage of development is called regression.
Play therapy	Play therapy is often used to help the diagnostician to try to determine the cause of disturbed behavior in a child. Treatment therapists then used a type of systematic desensitization or relearning therapy to change the disturbing behavior, either systematically or in less formal social settings.
Overt behavior	An action or response that is directly observable and measurable is an overt behavior.
Hyperactivity	Hyperactivity can be described as a state in which a individual is abnormally easily excitable and exuberant. Strong emotional reactions and a very short span of attention is also typical for the individual.
Temperament	Temperament refers to a basic, innate disposition to change behavior. The activity level is an important dimension of temperament.
Autism	Autism is a neurodevelopmental disorder that manifests itself in markedly abnormal social interaction, communication ability, patterns of interests, and patterns of behavior.

Go to **Cram101.com** for the Practice Tests for this Chapter.

Stages	Stages represent relatively discrete periods of time in which functioning is qualitatively different from functioning at other periods.
Self-report inventories	Personality tests that ask individuals to answer a series of questions about their own characteristic behaviors are called self-report inventories.
Face validity	Condition of testing in which test items appear plausible for their intended purposes is called face validity.
Syndrome	The term syndrome is the association of several clinically recognizable features, signs, symptoms, phenomena or characteristics which often occur together, so that the presence of one feature indicates the presence of the others.
Test reliability	Test Reliability is the extent to which a test is repeatable and yields consistent scores.
Simulation	A simulation is an imitation of some real device or state of affairs. Simulation attempts to represent certain features of the behavior of a physical or abstract system by the behavior of another system.
Incentive	An incentive is what is expected once a behavior is performed. An incentive acts as a reinforcer.
Chance variation	Differences between events without any known influence is considered a chance variation.
Cronbach	Cronbach is most famous for the development of Cronbach's alpha, a method for determining the reliability of educational and psychological tests. His work on test reliability reached an acme with the creation of generalizability theory, a statistical model for identifying and quantifying the sources of measurement error.
Predictive validity	Predictive validity refers to the relation between test scores and the student 's future performance .
Cross-validate	To cross-validate is to replicate the results of one sample with those of another sample.
Barnum effect	The Forer effect, or Barnum effect, is the observation that individuals will give high accuracy ratings to descriptions of their personality that supposedly are tailored specifically for them, but are in fact vague and general enough to apply to a wide range of people.
Survey	A method of scientific investigation in which a large sample of people answer questions about their attitudes or behavior is referred to as a survey.
Learning	Learning is a relatively permanent change in behavior that results from experience. Thus, to attribute a behavioral change to learning, the change must be relatively permanent and must result from experience.
Depersonaliz-tion	Depersonalization is the experience of feelings of loss of a sense of reality. A sufferer feels that they have changed and the world has become less real — it is vague, dreamlike, or lacking in significance.
Schizophrenia	Schizophrenia is characterized by persistent defects in the perception or expression of reality. A person suffering from untreated schizophrenia typically demonstrates grossly disorganized thinking, and may also experience delusions or auditory hallucinations
Personality trait	According to the Diagnostic and Statistical Manual of the American Psychiatric Association, a personality trait is a "prominent aspect of personality that is exhibited in a wide range of important social and personal contexts. ...".
Overt aggression	Aggression that is openly directed at its target is referred to as overt aggression.
Random sample	A sample drawn so that each member of a population has an equal chance of being selected to participate is referred to as a random sample.

Go to **Cram101.com** for the Practice Tests for this Chapter.

Punishment	Punishment is the addtion of a stimulus that reduces the frequency of a response, or the removal of a stimulus that results in a reduction of the response.
Ambiguous stimuli	Patterns that allow more than one perceptual organization are called ambiguous stimuli.
Projection	Attributing one's own undesirable thoughts, impulses, traits, or behaviors to others is referred to as projection.
Information Theory	Information Theory defines the notion of channel capacity and provides a mathematical model by which one can compute the maximal amount of information that can be carried by a channel.

144

Go to **Cram101.com** for the Practice Tests for this Chapter.

Personality	Personality refers to the pattern of enduring characteristics that differentiates a person, the patterns of behaviors that make each individual unique.
Construct	A generalized concept, such as anxiety or gravity, is a construct.
Personality type	A persistent style of complex behaviors defined by a group of related traits is referred to as a personality type. Myer Friedman and his co-workers first defined personality types in the 1950s. Friedman classified people into 2 categories, Type A and Type B.
Self-concept	Self-concept refers to domain-specific evaluations of the self where a domain may be academics, athletics, etc.
Naturalistic observation	Naturalistic observation is a method of observation that involves observing subjects in their natural habitats. Researchers take great care in avoiding making interferences with the behavior they are observing by using unobtrusive methods.
Attention	Attention is the cognitive process of selectively concentrating on one thing while ignoring other things. Psychologists have labeled three types of attention: sustained attention, selective attention, and divided attention.
Survey	A method of scientific investigation in which a large sample of people answer questions about their attitudes or behavior is referred to as a survey.
Psychological test	Psychological test refers to a standardized measure of a sample of a person's behavior.
Affective	Affective is the way people react emotionally, their ability to feel another living thing's pain or joy.
Variable	A variable refers to a measurable factor, characteristic, or attribute of an individual or a system.
Problem solving	An attempt to find an appropriate way of attaining a goal when the goal is not readily available is called problem solving.
Learning	Learning is a relatively permanent change in behavior that results from experience. Thus, to attribute a behavioral change to learning, the change must be relatively permanent and must result from experience.
Sternberg	Sternberg proposed the triarchic theory of intelligence: componential, experiential, and practical. His notion of general intelligence or the g-factor, is a composite of intelligence scores across multiple modalities.
Scheme	According to Piaget, a hypothetical mental structure that permits the classification and organization of new information is called a scheme.
Perception	Perception is the process of acquiring, interpreting, selecting, and organizing sensory information.
Thurstone	Thurstone was a pioneer in the field of psychometrics. His work in factor analysis led him to formulate a model of intelligence center around "Primary Mental Abilities", which were independent group factors of intelligence that different individuals possessed in varying degrees.
Rorschach	The Rorschach inkblot test is a method of psychological evaluation. It is a projective test associated with the Freudian school of thought. Psychologists use this test to try to probe the unconscious minds of their patients.
Personality trait	According to the Diagnostic and Statistical Manual of the American Psychiatric Association, a personality trait is a "prominent aspect of personality that is exhibited in a wide range of important social and personal contexts. ...".

Go to **Cram101.com** for the Practice Tests for this Chapter.

Trait	An enduring personality characteristic that tends to lead to certain behaviors is called a trait. The term trait also means a genetically inherited feature of an organism.
Adaptation	Adaptation is a lowering of sensitivity to a stimulus following prolonged exposure to that stimulus. Behavioral adaptations are special ways a particular organism behaves to survive in its natural habitat.
Spatial orientation	Spatial orientation refers to how people understand the placement of objects in space with themselves as the reference point.
Correlation	A statistical technique for determining the degree of association between two or more variables is referred to as correlation.
Performance-Based Assessment	Guidelines for using performance-based assessment cover four general issues: (1) establishing a clear purpose , (2) identifying observable criteria , (3) providing an appropriate setting , and (4) judging or scoring the performance .
Nomenclature	Nomenclature is a system of naming and categorizing objects in a given category.
Generalization	In conditioning, the tendency for a conditioned response to be evoked by stimuli that are similar to the stimulus to which the response was conditioned is a generalization. The greater the similarity among the stimuli, the greater the probability of generalization.
Temperament	Temperament refers to a basic, innate disposition to change behavior. The activity level is an important dimension of temperament.
Humors	The four humors were four fluids that were thought to permeate the body and influence its health. The concept was developed by ancient Greek thinkers around 400 BC and was directly linked with another popular theory of the four elements. Paired qualities were associated with each humour and its season.
Heuristic	A heuristic is a simple, efficient rule of thumb proposed to explain how people make decisions, come to judgments and solve problems, typically when facing complex problems or incomplete information. These rules work well under most circumstances, but in certain cases lead to systematic cognitive biases.
Kagan	The work of Kagan supports the concept of an inborn, biologically based temperamental predisposition to severe anxiety.
Myers-Briggs	The Myers-Briggs Type Indicator is a psychological test designed to assist a person in identifying their personality preferences. It follows from the theories of Carl Jung. The types tested for, known as dichotomies, are extraversion, introversion, sensing, intuition, thinking, feeling, judging and perceiving.
Dichotomy	A dichotomy is the division of a proposition into two parts which are both mutually exclusive – i.e. both cannot be simultaneously true – and jointly exhaustive – i.e. they cover the full range of possible outcomes. They are often contrasting and spoken of as "opposites".
Sensation	Sensation is the first stage in the chain of biochemical and neurologic events that begins with the impinging of a stimulus upon the receptor cells of a sensory organ, which then leads to perception, the mental state that is reflected in statements like "I see a uniformly blue wall."
Intuition	Quick, impulsive thought that does not make use of formal logic or clear reasoning is referred to as intuition.
Attitude	An enduring mental representation of a person, place, or thing that evokes an emotional response and related behavior is called attitude.
Jung	Jung was in some aspects a response to Sigmund Freud's psychoanalysis. He proposed and developed the concepts of the extroverted and introverted personality, archetypes, and the

Go to **Cram101.com** for the Practice Tests for this Chapter.

collective unconscious. His work has been influential in psychiatry and in the study of religion, literature, and related fields.

Premise	A premise is a statement presumed true within the context of a discourse, especially of a logical argument.
Psychometric	Psychometric study is concerned with the theory and technique of psychological measurement, which includes the measurement of knowledge, abilities, attitudes, and personality traits. The field is primarily concerned with the study of differences between individuals
Validity	The extent to which a test measures what it is intended to measure is called validity.
Questionnaire	A self-report method of data collection or clinical assessment method in which the individual being studied checks off items on a printed list, answers multiple-choice questions, or writes out answers to essay questions aimed at producing a selfdescription is called questionnaire.
Pupil	In the eye, the pupil is the opening in the middle of the iris. It appears black because most of the light entering it is absorbed by the tissues inside the eye. The size of the pupil is controlled by involuntary contraction and dilation of the iris, in order to regulate the intensity of light entering the eye. This is known as the pupillary reflex.
Altruism	Altruism is being helpful to other people with little or no interest in being rewarded for one's efforts. This is distinct from merely helping others.
Individual differences	Individual differences psychology studies the ways in which individual people differ in their behavior. This is distinguished from other aspects of psychology in that although psychology is ostensibly a study of individuals, modern psychologists invariably study groups.
Reliability	Reliability means the extent to which a test produces a consistent , reproducible score .
Leaderless group discussion	Leaderless group discussion is a form of leadership that simulates group decision making and problem solving.
Guilford	Guilford observed that most individuals display a preference for either convergent or divergent thinking. Scientists and engineers typically prefer the former and artists and performers, the latter.
Counselor	A counselor is a mental health professional who specializes in helping people with problems not involving serious mental disorders.
Stimulus	A change in an environmental condition that elicits a response is a stimulus.
Convergent validity	Convergent validity measures whether a test returns similar results to other tests which purport to measure the same or related constructs.
Resurgence	Resurgence refers to the reappearance during extinction, of a previously reinforced behavior.
Behavioral observation	A form of behavioral assessment that entails careful observation of a person's overt behavior in a particular situation is behavioral observation.
Theories	Theories are logically self-consistent models or frameworks describing the behavior of a certain natural or social phenomenon. They are broad explanations and predictions concerning phenomena of interest.
Variance	The degree to which scores differ among individuals in a distribution of scores is the variance.
Kohler	Kohler applied Gestalt principles to study chimpanzees and recorded their ability to devise and use tools and solve problems. In 1917, he published and gained fame with The Mentality of Apes, in which he argued that his subjects, like humans, were capable of insight learning.

Go to **Cram101.com** for the Practice Tests for this Chapter.

101

	His work led to a radical revision of learning theory.
Socioeconomic	Socioeconomic pertains to the study of the social and economic impacts of any product or service offering, market intervention or other activity on an economy as a whole and on the companies, organization and individuals who are its main economic actors.
Ego	In Freud's view the Ego serves to balance our primitive needs and our moral beliefs and taboos. Relying on experience, a healthy Ego provides the ability to adapt to reality and interact with the outside world.
Self-efficacy	Self-efficacy is the belief that one has the capabilities to execute the courses of actions required to manage prospective situations.
Self-esteem	Self-esteem refers to a person's subjective appraisal of himself or herself as intrinsically positive or negative to some degree.
Bandura	Bandura is best known for his work on social learning theory or Social Cognitivism. His famous Bobo doll experiment illustrated that people learn from observing others.
Self-image	A person's self-image is the mental picture, generally of a kind that is quite resistant to change, that depicts not only details that are potentially available to objective investigation by others, but also items that have been learned by that person about himself or herself.
Response set	A tendency to answer test items according to a personal or situational bias is called response set.
Empirical	Empirical means the use of working hypotheses which are capable of being disproved using observation or experiment.
Creativity	Creativity is the ability to think about something in novel and unusual ways and come up with unique solutions to problems. It involves divergent thinking, having many solutions or views to a problem.
Psychopathology	Psychopathology refers to the field concerned with the nature and development of mental disorders.
Narcissism	Narcissism is the pattern of thinking and behaving which involves infatuation and obsession with one's self to the exclusion of others.
Normal distribution	A normal distribution is a symmetrical distribution of scores that is assumed to reflect chance fluctuations; approximately 68% of cases lie within a single standard deviation of the mean.
Semantic differential	Semantic differential is a type of a rating scale designed to measure connotative meaning of objects, events, and concepts. A factor analysis of adjectives typically returns three factors: evaluation, potency, and activity.
Psychotherapy	Psychotherapy is a set of techniques based on psychological principles intended to improve mental health, emotional or behavioral issues.
Clinician	A health professional authorized to provide services to people suffering from one or more pathologies is a clinician.
Quantitative	A quantitative property is one that exists in a range of magnitudes, and can therefore be measured. Measurements of any particular quantitative property are expressed as as a specific quantity, referred to as a unit, multiplied by a number.
Social cognition	Social cognition is the name for both a branch of psychology that studies the cognitive processes involved in social interaction, and an umbrella term for the processes themselves. It uses the tools and assumptions of cognitive psychology to study how people understand

	themselves and others in society and social situations.
Cognition	The intellectual processes through which information is obtained, transformed, stored, retrieved, and otherwise used is cognition.
Constructivism	The view that individuals actively construct knowledge and understanding is referred to as constructivism.
Repertory Grid	Repertory Grid is an interviewing technique that complements the Theory of Personal Constructs. It aims to get people to talk about their construct system, and to identify the repertoire of constructs an individual typically uses to make sense of particular situations.
Population	Population refers to all members of a well-defined group of organisms, events, or things.
Positivism	Positivism is an approach to understanding the world based on science. It can be traced back to Auguste Comte in the 19th century. Positivists believe that there is little if any methodological difference between social sciences and natural sciences; societies, like nature, operate according to laws.
Autonomy	Autonomy is the condition of something that does not depend on anything else.
Clinical assessment	A clinical assessment is a systematic evaluation and measurement of psychological, biological, and social factors in a person presenting with a possible psychological disorder.
Standardized test	An oral or written assessment for which an individual receives a score indicating how the individual reponded relative to a previously tested large sample of others is referred to as a standardized test.
Direct observation	Direct observation refers to assessing behavior through direct surveillance.
Behavior modification	Behavior Modification is a technique of altering an individual's reactions to stimuli through positive reinforcement and the extinction of maladaptive behavior.
Social psychology	Social psychology is the study of the nature and causes of human social behavior, with an emphasis on how people think towards each other and how they relate to each other.
Adler	Adler argued that human personality could be explained teleologically, separate strands dominated by the guiding purpose of the individual's unconscious self ideal to convert feelings of inferiority to superiority (or rather completeness). The desires of the self ideal were countered by social and ethical demands.
Reid	Reid was the founder of the Scottish School of Common Sense, and played an integral role in the Scottish Enlightenment. He advocated direct realism, or common sense realism, and argued strongly against the Theory of Ideas advocated by John Locke and René Descartes.
Clinical psychology	Clinical psychology is involved in the diagnosis, assessment, and treatment of patients with mental or behavioral disorders, and conducts research in these various areas.
Structured interview	Structured interview refers to an interview in which the questions are set out in a prescribed fashion for the interviewer. It assists professionals in making diagnostic decisions based upon standardized criteria.
Halo effect	The halo effect occurs when a person's positive or negative traits seem to "spill over" from one area of their personality to another in others' perceptions of them.
Central tendency	In statistics, central tendency is an average of a set of measurements, the word average being variously construed as mean, median, or other measure of location, depending on the context. Central tendency is a descriptive statistic analogous to center of mass in physical terms.
Affect	A subjective feeling or emotional tone often accompanied by bodily expressions noticeable to

others is called affect.

Discrimination	In Learning theory, discrimination refers the ability to distinguish between a conditioned stimulus and other stimuli. It can be brought about by extensive training or differential reinforcement. In social terms, it is the denial of privileges to a person or a group on the basis of prejudice.
Applied psychology	The basic premise of applied psychology is the use of psychological principles and theories to overcome practical problems.
Halo error	The tendency for a rater to give an individual the same rating across different dimensions of performance is called the halo error.
Group structure	The network of roles, communication pathways, and power in a group is called the group structure.
Predictive validity	Predictive validity refers to the relation between test scores and the student 's future performance .
Content validity	The degree to which the content of a test is representative of the domain it's supposed to cover is referred to as its content validity.
Cognitive development	The process by which a child's understanding of the world changes as a function of age and experience is called cognitive development.
Clustering	Clustering is a technique used to enhance the memory by organization of conceptually-related categories.

Personality test	A personality test aims to describe aspects of a person's character that remain stable across situations.
Personality	Personality refers to the pattern of enduring characteristics that differentiates a person, the patterns of behaviors that make each individual unique.
Counselor	A counselor is a mental health professional who specializes in helping people with problems not involving serious mental disorders.
Achievement test	A test designed to determine a person's level of knowledge in a given subject area is referred to as an achievement test.
Standardized test	An oral or written assessment for which an individual receives a score indicating how the individual reponded relative to a previously tested large sample of others is referred to as a standardized test.
Intelligence test	An intelligence test is a standardized means of assessing a person's current mental ability, for example, the Stanford-Binet test and the Wechsler Adult Intelligence Scale.
Aptitude test	A test designed to predict a person's ability in a particular area or line of work is called an aptitude test.
Learning	Learning is a relatively permanent change in behavior that results from experience. Thus, to attribute a behavioral change to learning, the change must be relatively permanent and must result from experience.
Variable	A variable refers to a measurable factor, characteristic, or attribute of an individual or a system.
Scholastic Assessment Test	The Scholastic Assessment Test is a standardized test frequently used by colleges and universities to aid in the selection of incoming students.
Reasoning	Reasoning is the act of using reason to derive a conclusion from certain premises. There are two main methods to reach a conclusion,deductive reasoning and inductive reasoning.
Thorndike	Thorndike worked in animal behavior and the learning process leading to the theory of connectionism. Among his most famous contributions were his research on cats escaping from puzzle boxes, and his formulation of the Law of Effect.
Incentive value	The value of a goal above and beyond its ability to fill a need is its incentive value.
Incentive	An incentive is what is expected once a behavior is performed. An incentive acts as a reinforcer.
Attention	Attention is the cognitive process of selectively concentrating on one thing while ignoring other things. Psychologists have labeled three types of attention: sustained attention, selective attention, and divided attention.
Rote	Rote learning, is a learning technique which avoids grasping the inner complexities and inferences of the subject that is being learned and instead focuses on memorizing the material so that it can be recalled by the learner exactly the way it was read or heard.
Problem solving	An attempt to find an appropriate way of attaining a goal when the goal is not readily available is called problem solving.
Portfolio	A portfolio consists of a systematic and organized collection of a student 's work that demonstrates the student 's skills and accomplishments .
Performance-Based Assessment	Guidelines for using performance-based assessment cover four general issues: (1) establishing a clear purpose , (2) identifying observable criteria , (3) providing an appropriate setting , and (4) judging or scoring the performance .

Test anxiety	High levels of arousal and worry that seriously impair test performance is referred to as test anxiety.
Anxiety	Anxiety is a complex combination of the feeling of fear, apprehension and worry often accompanied by physical sensations such as palpitations, chest pain and/or shortness of breath.
Validity	The extent to which a test measures what it is intended to measure is called validity.
Trait	An enduring personality characteristic that tends to lead to certain behaviors is called a trait. The term trait also means a genetically inherited feature of an organism.
Predictive validity	Predictive validity refers to the relation between test scores and the student 's future performance .
Motivation	In psychology, motivation is the driving force (desire) behind all actions of an organism.
Cognitive skills	Cognitive skills such as reasoning, attention, and memory can be advanced and sustained through practice and training.
Attitude	An enduring mental representation of a person, place, or thing that evokes an emotional response and related behavior is called attitude.
Autonomy	Autonomy is the condition of something that does not depend on anything else.
Population	Population refers to all members of a well-defined group of organisms, events, or things.
Survey	A method of scientific investigation in which a large sample of people answer questions about their attitudes or behavior is referred to as a survey.
Psychometric	Psychometric study is concerned with the theory and technique of psychological measurement, which includes the measurement of knowledge, abilities, attitudes, and personality traits. The field is primarily concerned with the study of differences between individuals
Society	The social sciences use the term society to mean a group of people that form a semi-closed (or semi-open) social system, in which most interactions are with other individuals belonging to the group.
Reliability	Reliability means the extent to which a test produces a consistent , reproducible score .
Prototype	A concept of a category of objects or events that serves as a good example of the category is called a prototype.
Questionnaire	A self-report method of data collection or clinical assessment method in which the individual being studied checks off items on a printed list, answers multiple-choice questions, or writes out answers to essay questions aimed at producing a selfdescription is called questionnaire.
Variability	Statistically, variability refers to how much the scores in a distribution spread out, away from the mean.
Abnormal psychology	The scientific study whose objectives are to describe, explain, predict, and control behaviors that are considered strange or unusual is referred to as abnormal psychology.
Physiology	The study of the functions and activities of living cells, tissues, and organs and of the physical and chemical phenomena involved is referred to as physiology.
Anatomy	Anatomy is the branch of biology that deals with the structure and organization of living things. It can be divided into animal anatomy (zootomy) and plant anatomy (phytonomy). Major branches of anatomy include comparative anatomy, histology, and human anatomy.
Quantitative	A quantitative property is one that exists in a range of magnitudes, and can therefore be measured. Measurements of any particular quantitative property are expressed as as a specific

quantity, referred to as a unit, multiplied by a number.

Normative	The term normative is used to describe the effects of those structures of culture which regulate the function of social activity.
Case study	A carefully drawn biography that may be obtained through interviews, questionnaires, and psychological tests is called a case study.
Prognosis	A forecast about the probable course of an illess is referred to as prognosis.
Clinician	A health professional authorized to provide services to people suffering from one or more pathologies is a clinician.
Cognitive development	The process by which a child's understanding of the world changes as a function of age and experience is called cognitive development.
Early childhood	Early childhood refers to the developmental period extending from the end of infancy to about 5 or 6 years of age; sometimes called the preschool years.
Sensorimotor	The first of Piaget's stages is the Sensorimotor stage. This stage typically ranges from birth to 2 years. In this stage, children experience the world through their senses. During this stage, object permanence and stranger anxiety develop.
Maturation	The orderly unfolding of traits, as regulated by the genetic code is called maturation.
Acquisition	Acquisition is the process of adapting to the environment, learning or becoming conditioned. In classical conditoning terms, it is the initial learning of the stimulus response link, which involves a neutral stimulus being associated with a unconditioned stimulus and becoming a conditioned stimulus.
Discrimination	In Learning theory, discrimination refers the ability to distinguish between a conditioned stimulus and other stimuli. It can be brought about by extensive training or differential reinforcement. In social terms, it is the denial of privileges to a person or a group on the basis of prejudice.
Relational concept	A concept defined by the relationship between features of an object or between an object and its surroundings is a relational concept.
Empirical	Empirical means the use of working hypotheses which are capable of being disproved using observation or experiment.
Psychological test	Psychological test refers to a standardized measure of a sample of a person's behavior.
Cognitive psychology	Cognitive psychology is the psychological science which studies the mental processes that are hypothesised to underlie behavior. This covers a broad range of research domains, examining questions about the workings of memory, attention, perception, knowledge representation, reasoning, creativity and problem solving.
Affect	A subjective feeling or emotional tone often accompanied by bodily expressions noticeable to others is called affect.
Reading comprehension	Reading comprehension can be defined as the level of understanding of a passage or text. For normal reading rates (around 200-220 words per minute) an acceptable level of comprehension is above 75%.
Simulation	A simulation is an imitation of some real device or state of affairs. Simulation attempts to represent certain features of the behavior of a physical or abstract system by the behavior of another system.
Hull	Hull is best known for the Drive Reduction Theory which postulated that behavior occurs in response to primary drives such as hunger, thirst, sexual interest, etc. When the goal of the

drive is attained the drive is reduced. This reduction of drive serves as a reinforcer for learning.

Content validity	The degree to which the content of a test is representative of the domain it's supposed to cover is referred to as its content validity.
Adaptation	Adaptation is a lowering of sensitivity to a stimulus following prolonged exposure to that stimulus. Behavioral adaptations are special ways a particular organism behaves to survive in its natural habitat.
Construct	A generalized concept, such as anxiety or gravity, is a construct.
Feedback	Feedback refers to information returned to a person about the effects a response has had.
Industrial psychology	Industrial psychology is the study of the behavior of people in the workplace. Industrial psychology attempts to apply psychological results and methods to aid workers and organizations.
Validity generalization	A principle that states that if a predictor is a valid indicator of a criterion in one setting, it will be valid in another similar setting is the validity generalization.
Generalization	In conditioning, the tendency for a conditioned response to be evoked by stimuli that are similar to the stimulus to which the response was conditioned is a generalization. The greater the similarity among the stimuli, the greater the probability of generalization.
Paradigm	Paradigm refers to the set of practices that defines a scientific discipline during a particular period of time. It provides a framework from which to conduct research, it ensures that a certain range of phenomena, those on which the paradigm focuses, are explored thoroughly. Itmay also blind scientists to other, perhaps more fruitful, ways of dealing with their subject matter.
Individual differences	Individual differences psychology studies the ways in which individual people differ in their behavior. This is distinguished from other aspects of psychology in that although psychology is ostensibly a study of individuals, modern psychologists invariably study groups.
Antecedents	In behavior modification, events that typically precede the target response are called antecedents.
Personality trait	According to the Diagnostic and Statistical Manual of the American Psychiatric Association, a personality trait is a "prominent aspect of personality that is exhibited in a wide range of important social and personal contexts. ...".
Sternberg	Sternberg proposed the triarchic theory of intelligence: componential, experiential, and practical. His notion of general intelligence or the g-factor, is a composite of intelligence scores across multiple modalities.
Life stages	Widely recognized periods of life corresponding to broad phases of development are called life stages. They may cross-culturally or socially defined.
Stages	Stages represent relatively discrete periods of time in which functioning is qualitatively different from functioning at other periods.
Correlation	A statistical technique for determining the degree of association between two or more variables is referred to as correlation.
Norms	In testing, standards of test performance that permit the comparison of one person's score on the test to the scores of others who have taken the same test are referred to as norms.
Information processing	Information processing is an approach to the goal of understanding human thinking. The essence of the approach is to see cognition as being essentially computational in nature, with mind being the software and the brain being the hardware.

Go to **Cram101.com** for the Practice Tests for this Chapter.

Test battery	A group of tests and interviews given to the same individual is a test battery.
Representative sample	Representative sample refers to a sample of participants selected from the larger population in such a way that important subgroups within the population are included in the sample in the same proportions as they are found in the larger population.
Coding	In senation, coding is the process by which information about the quality and quantity of a stimulus is preserved in the pattern of action potentials sent through sensory neurons to the central nervous system.
Variance	The degree to which scores differ among individuals in a distribution of scores is the variance.
Spatial visualization	An aspect of spatial cognition that involves the mental manipulations of visual stimuli, such as performing mental rotation or solving embedded-figures problems is referred to as spatial visualization.
Factor analysis	Factor analysis is a statistical technique that originated in psychometrics. The objective is to explain the most of the variability among a number of observable random variables in terms of a smaller number of unobservable random variables called factors.
Intrapersonal	Intrapersonal is the ability to recognize, define, and pursue inner feelings and thoughts, as in poetry and self-knowledge.
Mayer	Mayer developed the concept of emotional intelligence with Peter Salovey. He is one of the authors of the Mayer-Salovey-Caruso Emotional Intelligence Test, and has developed a new, integrated framework for personality psychology, known as the Systems Framework for Pesronality Psychology.
Meta-analysis	In statistics, a meta-analysis combines the results of several studies that address a set of related research hypotheses.
Modeling	A type of behavior learned through observation of others demonstrating the same behavior is modeling.
Conscientiou-ness	Conscientiousness is one of the dimensions of the five-factor model of personality and individual differences involving being organized, thorough, and reliable as opposed to careless, negligent, and unreliable.
Five-factor model	The five-factor model of personality proposes that there are five universal dimensions of personality: Neuroticism, Extraversion, Openness, Conscientiousness, and Agreeableness.
Industrial and organizational psychology	Industrial and organizational psychology is the study of the behavior of people in the workplace. Industrial and organizational psychology attempts to apply psychological results and methods to aid workers and organizations.
Theories	Theories are logically self-consistent models or frameworks describing the behavior of a certain natural or social phenomenon. They are broad explanations and predictions concerning phenomena of interest.
Agreeableness	Agreeableness, one of the big-five personality traits, reflects individual differences in concern with cooperation and social harmony. It is the degree individuals value getting along with others.
Polygraph	A polygraph is a device which measures and records several physiological variables such as blood pressure, heart rate, respiration and skin conductivity while a series of questions is being asked, in an attempt to detect lies.
American Psychological Association	The American Psychological Association is a professional organization representing psychology in the US. The mission statement is to "advance psychology as a science and profession and as a means of promoting health, education , and human welfare".

Applied psychology	The basic premise of applied psychology is the use of psychological principles and theories to overcome practical problems.
Self-report inventories	Personality tests that ask individuals to answer a series of questions about their own characteristic behaviors are called self-report inventories.
Personality inventory	A self-report questionnaire by which an examinee indicates whether statements assessing habitual tendencies apply to him or her is referred to as a personality inventory.
Kohler	Kohler applied Gestalt principles to study chimpanzees and recorded their ability to devise and use tools and solve problems. In 1917, he published and gained fame with The Mentality of Apes, in which he argued that his subjects, like humans, were capable of insight learning. His work led to a radical revision of learning theory.
Counseling psychologist	A doctoral level mental health professional whose training is similar to that of a clinical psychologist, though usually with less emphasis on research and serious psychopathology is referred to as a counseling psychologist.
Individual intelligence test	A test of intelligence designed to be given to a single individual by a trained specialist is an individual intelligence test. Background information supplements the test.
Wechsler Scales	The Wechsler Scales are two well-known intelligence scales, namely the Wechsler Adult Intelligence Scale and the Wechsler Intelligence Scale for Children.
Clinical psychologist	A psychologist, usually with a Ph.D, whose training is in the diagnosis, treatment, or research of psychological and behavioral disorders is a clinical psychologist.
Forensic psychology	Psychological research and theory that deals with the effects of cognitive, affective, and behavioral factors on legal proceedings and the law is a forensic psychology.
Health psychology	The field of psychology that studies the relationships between psychological factors and the prevention and treatment of physical illness is called health psychology.
Neuropsychology	Neuropsychology is a branch of psychology that aims to understand how the structure and function of the brain relates to specific psychological processes.
Adler	Adler argued that human personality could be explained teleologically, separate strands dominated by the guiding purpose of the individual's unconscious self ideal to convert feelings of inferiority to superiority (or rather completeness). The desires of the self ideal were countered by social and ethical demands.
Brain	The brain controls and coordinates most movement, behavior and homeostatic body functions such as heartbeat, blood pressure, fluid balance and body temperature. Functions of the brain are responsible for cognition, emotion, memory, motor learning and other sorts of learning. The brain is primarily made up of two types of cells: glia and neurons.
Hypothesis	A specific statement about behavior or mental processes that is testable through research is a hypothesis.
Developmental psychology	The branch of psychology that studies the patterns of growth and change occurring throughout life is referred to as developmental psychology.
Stanford-Binet	Terman released the "Stanford Revision of the Binet-Simon Scale" or the Stanford-Binet for short. Using validation experiments, he removed several of the Binet-Simon test items and added new ones. In 1985 it was revised to analyze an individual's responses in four content areas: verbal reasoning, quantitative reasoning, abstract reasoning, and short-term memory.
Psychopathology	Psychopathology refers to the field concerned with the nature and development of mental disorders.

Go to **Cram101.com** for the Practice Tests for this Chapter.

Personality disorder	A mental disorder characterized by a set of inflexible, maladaptive personality traits that keep a person from functioning properly in society is referred to as a personality disorder.
Donders	Donders discovered that farsightedness was caused by too shallow an eyeball and that astigmatism was caused by uneven curvature of the cornea or lens.
Clinical significance	The degree to which research findings have useful and meaningful applications to real problems is called their clinical significance.
Perception	Perception is the process of acquiring, interpreting, selecting, and organizing sensory information.
Trauma	Trauma refers to a severe physical injury or wound to the body caused by an external force, or a psychological shock having a lasting effect on mental life.
Elaboration	The extensiveness of processing at any given level of memory is called elaboration. The use of elaboration changes developmentally. Adolescents are more likely to use elaboration spontaneously than children.
Syndrome	The term syndrome is the association of several clinically recognizable features, signs, symptoms, phenomena or characteristics which often occur together, so that the presence of one feature indicates the presence of the others.
Right hemisphere	The brain is divided into left and right cerebral hemispheres. The right hemisphere of the cortex controls the left side of the body.
Lesion	A lesion is a non-specific term referring to abnormal tissue in the body. It can be caused by any disease process including trauma (physical, chemical, electrical), infection, neoplasm, metabolic and autoimmune.
Pathology	Pathology is the study of the processes underlying disease and other forms of illness, harmful abnormality, or dysfunction.
Age effects	Beahvioral consequences of being aware of one's chronological age are referred to as age effects.
Physiological changes	Alterations in heart rate, blood pressure, perspiration, and other involuntary responses are physiological changes.
Depressive disorders	Depressive disorders are mood disorders in which the individual suffers depression without ever experiencing mania.
Depression	In everyday language depression refers to any downturn in mood, which may be relatively transitory and perhaps due to something trivial. This is differentiated from Clinical depression which is marked by symptoms that last two weeks or more and are so severe that they interfere with daily living.
Dementia	Dementia is progressive decline in cognitive function due to damage or disease in the brain beyond what might be expected from normal aging.
Organicity	Damage or deterioration in the central nervous system is called organicity.
Presenting problem	The presenting problem is the original complaint reported by the client to the therapist. The actual treated problem may sometimes be a modification derived from the presenting problem or entirely different..
Neuropsychol-gist	A psychologist concerned with the relationships among cognition, affect, behavior, and brain function is a neuropsychologist.
Raw score	A raw score is an original datum that has not been transformed – for example, the original result obtained by a student on a test (i.e., the number of correctly answered items) as opposed to that score after transformation to a standard score or percentile rank or the

like.

Positron emission tomography	Positron Emission Tomography measures emissions from radioactively labeled chemicals that have been injected into the bloodstream. The greatest benefit is that different compounds can show blood flow and oxygen and glucose metabolism in the tissues of the working brain.
Magnetic resonance imaging	Magnetic resonance imaging is a method of creating images of the inside of opaque organs in living organisms as well as detecting the amount of bound water in geological structures. It is primarily used to demonstrate pathological or other physiological alterations of living tissues and is a commonly used form of medical imaging.
Electroencep-alography	Electroencephalography is the neurophysiologic measurement of the electrical activity of the brain by recording from electrodes placed on the scalp, or in special cases on the cortex. The resulting traces are known as an electroencephalogram (EEG) and represent so-called brainwaves.
Neuroimaging	Neuroimaging comprises all invasive, minimally invasive, and non-invasive methods for obtaing structural and functional images of the nervous system's major subsystems: the brain, the peripheral nervous system, and the spinal cord.
Neurologist	A physician who studies the nervous system, especially its structure, functions, and abnormalities is referred to as neurologist.
Learning disability	A learning disability exists when there is a significant discrepancy between one's ability and achievement.
Dyslexia	Dyslexia is a neurological disorder with biochemical and genetic markers. In its most common and apparent form, it is a disability in which a person's reading and/or writing ability is significantly lower than that which would be predicted by his or her general level of intelligence.
Aphasia	Aphasia is a loss or impairment of the ability to produce or comprehend language, due to brain damage. It is usually a result of damage to the language centers of the brain.
Mental retardation	Mental retardation refers to having significantly below-average intellectual functioning and limitations in at least two areas of adaptive functioning. Many categorize retardation as mild, moderate, severe, or profound.
Heterogeneous	A heterogeneous compound, mixture, or other such object is one that consists of many different items, which are often not easily sorted or separated, though they are clearly distinct.
Encoding	Encoding refers to interpreting; transforming; modifying information so that it can be placed in memory. It is the first stage of information processing.
Short-term memory	Short-term memory is that part of memory which stores a limited amount of information for a limited amount of time (roughly 30-45 seconds). The second key concept associated with a short-term memory is that it has a finite capacity.
Moderate mental retardation	Moderate mental retardation is a limitation in mental development. Scores on IQ tests range between 35-50. People with this degree of retardation are often institutionalized, and their training is focused on self-care rather than on development of intellectual skills.
Giftedness	Either the possession of a high IQ, special talents or aptitudes is called giftedness.
Generalizability	The ability to extend a set of findings observed in one piece of research to other situations and groups is called generalizability.
Threshold	In general, a threshold is a fixed location or value where an abrupt change is observed. In the sensory modalities, it is the minimum amount of stimulus energy necessary to elicit a sensory response.

Go to **Cram101.com** for the Practice Tests for this Chapter.

Behavioral assessment	Direct measures of an individual's behavior used to describe characteristics indicative of personality are called behavioral assessment.
Behavior modification	Behavior Modification is a technique of altering an individual's reactions to stimuli through positive reinforcement and the extinction of maladaptive behavior.
Clinical psychology	Clinical psychology is involved in the diagnosis, assessment, and treatment of patients with mental or behavioral disorders, and conducts research in these various areas.
Statistics	Statistics is a type of data analysis which practice includes the planning, summarizing, and interpreting of observations of a system possibly followed by predicting or forecasting of future events based on a mathematical model of the system being observed.
Statistic	A statistic is an observable random variable of a sample.
Conditioning	Conditioning describes the process by which behaviors can be learned or modified through interaction with the environment.
Behavior therapy	Behavior therapy refers to the systematic application of the principles of learning to direct modification of a client's problem behaviors.
Affective	Affective is the way people react emotionally, their ability to feel another living thing's pain or joy.
Bandura	Bandura is best known for his work on social learning theory or Social Cognitivism. His famous Bobo doll experiment illustrated that people learn from observing others.
Phobia	A persistent, irrational fear of an object, situation, or activity that the person feels compelled to avoid is referred to as a phobia.
Direct observation	Direct observation refers to assessing behavior through direct surveillance.
Sexual arousal disorders	Problems occurring during the excitement phase and relating to difficulties with feelings of sexual pleasure or with the physiological changes associated with sexual excitement are called sexual arousal disorders.
Beck Depression Inventory	The Beck Depression Inventory is a 21 question multiple choice survey that is one of the most widely used instruments for measuring depression severity.
Structured interview	Structured interview refers to an interview in which the questions are set out in a prescribed fashion for the interviewer. It assists professionals in making diagnostic decisions based upon standardized criteria.
Social skills	Social skills are skills used to interact and communicate with others to assist status in the social structure and other motivations.
Temperament	Temperament refers to a basic, innate disposition to change behavior. The activity level is an important dimension of temperament.
Blocking	If the one of the two members of a compound stimulus fails to produce the CR due to an earlier conditioning of the other member of the compound stimulus, blocking has occurred.
Cognition	The intellectual processes through which information is obtained, transformed, stored, retrieved, and otherwise used is cognition.
Stereotype	A stereotype is considered to be a group concept, held by one social group about another. They are often used in a negative or prejudicial sense and are frequently used to justify certain discriminatory behaviors. This allows powerful social groups to legitimize and protect their dominant position
Algorithm	A systematic procedure for solving a problem that works invariably when it is correctly

Go to **Cram101.com** for the Practice Tests for this Chapter.

Go to **Cram101.com** for the Practice Tests for this Chapter.
And, **NEVER** highlight a book again!

	applied is called an algorithm.
Clinical method	Studying psychological problems and therapies in clinical settings is referred to as the clinical method. It usually involves case histories, pathology, or non-experimentally controlled environments.
Barnum effect	The Forer effect, or Barnum effect, is the observation that individuals will give high accuracy ratings to descriptions of their personality that supposedly are tailored specifically for them, but are in fact vague and general enough to apply to a wide range of people.
Reaction time	The amount of time required to respond to a stimulus is referred to as reaction time.
Psychological testing	Psychological testing is a field characterized by the use of small samples of behavior in order to infer larger generalizations about a given individual. The technical term for psychological testing is psychometrics.
Life satisfaction	A person's attitudes about his or her overall life are referred to as life satisfaction.

Empirical	Empirical means the use of working hypotheses which are capable of being disproved using observation or experiment.
Psychotherapy	Psychotherapy is a set of techniques based on psychological principles intended to improve mental health, emotional or behavioral issues.
Personality	Personality refers to the pattern of enduring characteristics that differentiates a person, the patterns of behaviors that make each individual unique.
Psychological test	Psychological test refers to a standardized measure of a sample of a person's behavior.
Attention	Attention is the cognitive process of selectively concentrating on one thing while ignoring other things. Psychologists have labeled three types of attention: sustained attention, selective attention, and divided attention.
Psychological testing	Psychological testing is a field characterized by the use of small samples of behavior in order to infer larger generalizations about a given individual. The technical term for psychological testing is psychometrics.
Applied psychology	The basic premise of applied psychology is the use of psychological principles and theories to overcome practical problems.
Industrial and organizational psychology	Industrial and organizational psychology is the study of the behavior of people in the workplace. Industrial and organizational psychology attempts to apply psychological results and methods to aid workers and organizations.
Standardized test	An oral or written assessment for which an individual receives a score indicating how the individual reponded relative to a previously tested large sample of others is referred to as a standardized test.
Society	The social sciences use the term society to mean a group of people that form a semi-closed (or semi-open) social system, in which most interactions are with other individuals belonging to the group.
Aptitude test	A test designed to predict a person's ability in a particular area or line of work is called an aptitude test.
Test battery	A group of tests and interviews given to the same individual is a test battery.
Affect	A subjective feeling or emotional tone often accompanied by bodily expressions noticeable to others is called affect.
Inference	Inference is the act or process of drawing a conclusion based solely on what one already knows.
Psychometric	Psychometric study is concerned with the theory and technique of psychological measurement, which includes the measurement of knowledge, abilities, attitudes, and personality traits. The field is primarily concerned with the study of differences between individuals
Prototype	A concept of a category of objects or events that serves as a good example of the category is called a prototype.
Individual intelligence test	A test of intelligence designed to be given to a single individual by a trained specialist is an individual intelligence test. Background information supplements the test.
Intelligence test	An intelligence test is a standardized means of assessing a person's current mental ability, for example, the Stanford-Binet test and the Wechsler Adult Intelligence Scale.
Personality test	A personality test aims to describe aspects of a person's character that remain stable across situations.

Go to **Cram101.com** for the Practice Tests for this Chapter.

Norms	In testing, standards of test performance that permit the comparison of one person's score on the test to the scores of others who have taken the same test are referred to as norms.
Trait	An enduring personality characteristic that tends to lead to certain behaviors is called a trait. The term trait also means a genetically inherited feature of an organism.
Achievement test	A test designed to determine a person's level of knowledge in a given subject area is referred to as an achievement test.
Ideology	An ideology can be thought of as a comprehensive vision, as a way of looking at things, as in common sense and several philosophical tendencies, or a set of ideas proposed by the dominant class of a society to all members of this society.
Informed consent	The term used by psychologists to indicate that a person has agreed to participate in research after receiving information about the purposes of the study and the nature of the treatments is informed consent. Even with informed consent, subjects may withdraw from any experiment at any time.
Validity	The extent to which a test measures what it is intended to measure is called validity.
Counselor	A counselor is a mental health professional who specializes in helping people with problems not involving serious mental disorders.
Psychiatrist	A psychiatrist is a physician who specializes in the diagnosis and treatment of psychological disorders.
Learning	Learning is a relatively permanent change in behavior that results from experience. Thus, to attribute a behavioral change to learning, the change must be relatively permanent and must result from experience.
Feedback	Feedback refers to information returned to a person about the effects a response has had.
Habit	A habit is a response that has become completely separated from its eliciting stimulus. Early learning theorists used the term to describe S-R associations, however not all S-R associations become a habit, rather many are extinguished after reinforcement is withdrawn.
Counseling psychologist	A doctoral level mental health professional whose training is similar to that of a clinical psychologist, though usually with less emphasis on research and serious psychopathology is referred to as a counseling psychologist.
Population	Population refers to all members of a well-defined group of organisms, events, or things.
Statistics	Statistics is a type of data analysis which practice includes the planning, summarizing, and interpreting of observations of a system possibly followed by predicting or forecasting of future events based on a mathematical model of the system being observed.
Statistic	A statistic is an observable random variable of a sample.
Motivation	In psychology, motivation is the driving force (desire) behind all actions of an organism.
Attitude	An enduring mental representation of a person, place, or thing that evokes an emotional response and related behavior is called attitude.
Discrimination	In Learning theory, discrimination refers the ability to distinguish between a conditioned stimulus and other stimuli. It can be brought about by extensive training or differential reinforcement. In social terms, it is the denial of privileges to a person or a group on the basis of prejudice.
Empirical evidence	Facts or information based on direct observation or experience are referred to as empirical evidence.
Reasoning	Reasoning is the act of using reason to derive a conclusion from certain premises. There are

Go to **Cram101.com** for the Practice Tests for this Chapter.

two main methods to reach a conclusion,deductive reasoning and inductive reasoning.

Stereotype	A stereotype is considered to be a group concept, held by one social group about another.They are often used in a negative or prejudicial sense and are frequently used to justify certain discriminatory behaviors. This allows powerful social groups to legitimize and protect their dominant position
Normative	The term normative is used to describe the effects of those structures of culture which regulate the function of social activity.
Paranoid	The term paranoid is typically used in a general sense to signify any self-referential delusion, or more specifically, to signify a delusion involving the fear of persecution.
Innate	Innate behavior is not learned or influenced by the environment, rather, it is present or predisposed at birth.
Prejudice	Prejudice in general, implies coming to a judgment on the subject before learning where the preponderance of the evidence actually lies, or formation of a judgement without direct experience.
Portfolio	A portfolio consists of a systematic and organized collection of a student 's work that demonstrates the student 's skills and accomplishments .

Go to **Cram101.com** for the Practice Tests for this Chapter.

Printed in the United States
67495LVS00002B/181-186